Dedication

Written with the sincerest love for all the dear brothers and sisters, for all the wonderful Jehovah's Witnesses to help them leave the Watchtower with no harm to themselves and to their families.

— ••●•• —

— ··•·· —

How to Leave Jehovah's Witnesses with No Harm to Yourself and to Your Family

–

Your Exit Manual

Dan Bergher

— ··•·· —

Table of Contents

How Can This Book Help You and How Is It Unique?

You want to leave the Watchtower, and you want to help your family members who are Jehovah's Witnesses to leave the Watchtower together with you.

This Exit Manual will show you many aspects of how to plan and execute your exit steps to keep your relationships with no harm or with as little harm as possible.

This book will be guiding you step by step if you want to leave Jehovah's Witnesses but among them you still have:

Your spouse, children, family members and loved ones,

Your friends, acquaintances and neighbors,

Your job partners and work related relationships.

I know how you feel: I was one of Jehovah's Witnesses for 25 years. Hundreds of sisters and brothers have been helped by me personally, using these methods. And now, all these methods are available to everybody in this book.

Read this book as a conversation with a close friend who wants to help you make a smooth exit together with your family and conduct your life in freedom.

This book will also be helpful if:

You are a professional therapist, counselor or minister working with Jehovah's Witnesses who are leaving their religion.

In Which Areas Will This Book Help You?

You don't need to lose your loved ones when leaving the Watchtower.

Among other things, this book will help you in the following areas:

* Five ways to disprove that there was no "governing body" in the first century C.E., just from the New World Translation (NWT). Once JWs see there was no "governing body," it is easier for them to leave.

* Five exit strategies: How to choose from them.

* Disprove the teaching about the year 1914, just from the NWT.

- Dismantle the authority of the Watchtower without using any "apostate" literature.
- How to talk to your JW spouse and family members to gain them.
- How to protect your children.
- How to handle a situation in which your spouse already views you as an apostate and wants a separation or divorce.
- How there's no danger in staying inside JWs if you know what to do and if you are staying because of your family members.
- How you can be of much more help to your JW spouse and family if you are still viewed as a faithful JW member.
- How to use a ruse in your exit strategy.
- How to behave during meetings and how to talk to the elders.
- How to behave in the case of a judicial committee.
- How to view the things that you have given to the Watchtower.
- How to mitigate the effects of your exit from the Watchtower.
- How to make new friends.
- How to leave without holding a grudge and with peace of mind.

* * *

Imagine you leave the Watchtower in a rash, hasty way. You are out. But your spouse, your children, your parents, grandparents, family members, friends and acquaintances stayed in. What are the consequences of such an approach?

Your relationships with your family members will be under a huge amount of stress. Because of indoctrination by the Watchtower, they will see you as an **apostate**; as a **threat** to their spiritual well-being.

You definitely don't want anything like that in your life!

I've heard of marriages that ended abruptly after one of the spouses left the Watchtower (WT).

I've heard of fathers and mothers who left the WT but who cannot speak with their grown-up children who are still JWs.

I've heard of grown-up children who left the WT but who cannot speak with their father and mother who are still JWs.

I've heard of grandparents who left the WT but who cannot speak with their children and grandchildren who are still JWs.

Leave With No Harm and With Peace of Mind

On the other hand, I have personally helped hundreds of dear Sisters and Brothers in choosing a patient, well thought-out exit strategy. They left the organization, but their marriage stayed intact; their relationships with their family members stayed intact too.

How did they do it?

They used one of the approaches described in this book.

I will do my best to lead you "by the hand" in this book. Among your goals could be to:

Have your family members on your side.

Live in a peaceful relationship with God.

Forgive and hold no grudges.

See the past with no regrets, learn from it and move on.

Start a new journey to grow and heal.

— ••●•• —

How to Read This Book

I presume that you will start with the detailed Table of Contents and jump right into a topic that is the most important for you right now. To get an overall picture of all the methods and strategies and to weigh all the options, you might also want to read the book from cover to cover. In case you don't, the most important principles are stressed repeatedly.

Journaling

Journaling could be very helpful. This can be a physical paper journal or a notepad. Alternatively, you can choose an application (e.g. on your smartphone) that you might even protect with a password.

Note down the current date, your observations and any ToDo's and ideas you want to start applying right away. The things in your life will be moving forward, and later you will see that the time has come to use another, perhaps more advanced strategy from this book.

Thanks to your notes, you will see things more clearly and you might be able to help your family members and your friends much better.

Two Types of Helpful Tasks for You

There are two types of helpful tasks for you at the end of each part in this book. These tasks are designed to make the exit smooth both for you and for your JW family members together with you.

TASK #1: ✱ Understanding the Main Points

Questions to help reassure you about the main points from the chapter.

Example

Q: What one thing will the elders want to see from you during the judicial committee?

A: Repentance. (Even if it's just a ruse. I need to stay inside the organization to help my JW family members get out.) <An example of a specific point from the chapter.>

TASK #2: ✱ Taking My Time to Reflect <Ask 10–100 times>

Reflective questions to help you find out new possibilities, new ways of thinking about things.

These questions should help you find the best steps for your current situation.

Examples

- How can I make this as easy as possible? For me, my spouse, my family, for …
- What will create more here? For me, my spouse, my family, for …
- What possibilities are there?
- What other questions can help me?
- Which approach/decision feels lighter/heavier?
- Which approach/decision feels expanding/limiting?

Your Goal

You want to help your JW family members to leave the Watchtower together with you—with no harm to yourself, with no harm to your family.

You can choose only the question(s) that speak to you at this time.

Example

Let's see how you can use these reflective questions when deciding **which of the five exit strategies to use**.

Q: Which approach (exit strategy 1, 2, 3, 4 or 5) will create more here?

Q: Which decision will create more here?

Q: What will create more here: For me? For my spouse? For our marriage? For our children? For our family? For our parents? For our relatives? For…?

Q: Which approach feels lighter? Which approach feels heavier?

Q: Which approach feels expanding? Which approach feels limiting?

ASK 10 to 100 Times

Don't hurry. Get back to the same question tomorrow, in a week, etc.

The best is to put these reflective questions into a loop. Ask the same question 10–100 times.

Answers

There are no general right or wrong answers. These "reflective" questions will help you find **the best answers for your own current situation**.

TIP: After reading a chapter, write down the chosen "reflective" question(s) into your journal or on a piece of paper and reflect on it during the day—10 times, 50 times, 100 times. Only then, you will be pleasantly surprised with what you will find out and what kind of peace you will start experiencing. You will be surprised by how many good things will start happening in your life!

— ••●•• —

Your Loyalty, Double Life, Using a Ruse

Briefly: How to use a ruse to protect yourself and your family when leaving the Watchtower.

The Watchtower uses all these terms to its own advantage, to control their members; to keep them in check.

Loyalty: According to the Watchtower, "loyalty to God also includes loyalty to his organization," together with any "corrections and adjustments to our understanding." [w01 10/1 pp. 20-23] Interestingly, the WT doesn't have to be loyal to its own teaching; it can be changed, as needed.

Double Life: "Leading a double life is a serious offense against God." [w88 8/1 pp. 16-21] Interestingly, the WT can say one thing to its members (e.g. about blood transfusions) and a different thing to the general public.

Ruse: 'Misdirecting those who have no right to the truth.' Not telling the truth to those who do not have the right to the truth. [w13 11/1 p. 14-15] According to the WT, the state officials do not have the right to the truth:

For example, to gain legal recognition in some countries (e.g. in the Eastern Europe), the Watchtower representatives stated that Jehovah's Witnesses do not teach their members to "abstain from blood" transfusions. The organization told its members that it was necessary to resort to a ruse to be granted legal recognition.

You can and you should start using these approaches to your advantage right now.

Ruse: Learning From Rahab

This approach is praised in the Watchtower many times over, as we can see below.

The Bible book of Joshua shows how **Rahab used a ruse**, a simple **strategy**, when "she had misdirected murderous men who had no right to the truth, and she had saved innocent servants of Jehovah."

> "Rahab had little time to think, yet she was resourceful and acted quickly. She had the spies hide among stalks of flax that were laid out to dry on the flat roof of her house. Then she spoke to the king's messengers, saying:

'Yes, the men did come to me, and I did not know from where they were. And it came about at the closing of the gate by dark that the men went out. I just do not know where the men have gone. Chase after them quickly, for you will overtake them.' (Joshua 2:4, 5) Imagine Rahab watching the faces of the king's emissaries. Did she wonder if they could tell that her heart was racing? **Her ruse worked!** The king's men hurried off in the direction of the fords of the Jordan. (Joshua 2:7) Rahab must have breathed a quiet sigh of relief. Using a simple **strategy**, she had misdirected murderous men who had **no right to the truth** and she had **saved innocent servants** of Jehovah." [w13 11/1 p. 14-15; emphasis added]

According to the Watchtower:

- Rahab was not lying; she *used a ruse*, "simple strategy".

- Rahab used a ruse to misdirect men who had *no right to the truth*.

- This way, Rahab *saved innocent servants* of Jehovah.

Lying and Ruse According to the Watchtower

Lying: *Not telling the truth to those who have the right to the truth.*

To serve the WT's means, supposedly only the organization has the right to the truth which extends to loyal elders within the organization (the elders have the right to hear the truth from you and you have to tell them the truth).

Ruse: *Not telling the truth to those who do not have the right to the truth.*

A ruse can be freely used with those who are against the WT; not telling them the truth does not constitute lying, it means using a ruse.

Back to Rahab.

Rahab is praised both in the Bible and in the publications of the WT. She is one of the four women named in Matthew's genealogy of Jesus. (Mt 1:5-6; Ru 4:20-22)

It is extremely important to understand the story of Rahab. This will make your life much, much easier when leaving JWs. Please, take your Bible and read the whole narrative from the book of Joshua 2:1-21; 6:17-25.

Let's stress what the Watchtower says about Rahab:

> **"Rahab's ruse worked! ... Using a simple strategy, she had misdirected men who had no right to the truth and she had saved innocent servants of Jehovah."**

What to Take Away From This?

You do not have to subscribe to WT's definition of terms. Their definitions serve only their own purposes, to keep you within the organization, to impute the feelings of guilt, to manipulate you and to keep you in check.

It is clear that the Watchtower shows the ruse that was used by Rahab in positive terms.

There are way more examples:

Gibeonites: Resorting to a ruse, the Gibeonites sent representatives who posed as travelers from a distant land. (Joshua 9:3-27; 10:1-14)

Jehu: By the ruse of calling a great gathering for the worship of Baal, Jehu got all of Israel's Baal worshipers to assemble at the house of Baal. This way Jehu annihilated Baal out of Israel. (2Ki 10:18-28)

Joseph: Joseph had his silver cup placed in Benjamin's bag, which was part of his ruse. (Ge 44:1-5)

Laban and Leah: Laban used a ruse with Jacob by giving him Leah as a wife instead of Rachel. Leah consented to be a part of this ruse. (Ge 29:18-28)

Rebekah: Rebekah disguises Jacob so that Jacob secures the blessing from his father for himself. (Ge 27:1-17, 29; 28:3, 4)

See more in the Appendix, "Ruse: More Details."

If we stay with Rahab, it is clear that according to the Bible and the Watchtower, Rahab did a praiseworthy thing:

>**Rahab used a ruse,**
>
>**to misdirect men who had no right to the truth,**
>
>**to save herself, her loved ones and all her relatives.**

Be Like Rahab: Ruse in Your Life

It might bring you peace of mind to define the term in the following way:

>**Ruse:** Not telling the truth to those who *do not have the right* to the truth at this time: those who would do harm to you, to your spouse, to your family, to your loved ones; misdirecting these people means using a ruse. You can misdirect and mislead people like this by giving them a false impression. You can freely use a ruse with anybody who could harm you or your loved ones in any way, to protect yourself and your family.

You can even make "ruse" more personal:

>**Ruse:** "I don't have to tell the truth to those who *do not have the right* to the truth at this time: to those who would do harm to me, to my spouse, to

my family, to my loved ones. I can and I should misdirect these people using a ruse. I can misdirect and mislead people like this by giving them a false impression. I can freely use a ruse with anybody who could harm me or my loved ones in any way, to protect myself and my family."

What Is Your End?

Your end is to leave the Watchtower with no harm to yourself, to your spouse, to your marriage, to your family, relatives, friends. You want your family to stay intact; you want to keep your friends.

You can and you should use a ruse to protect yourself and your family.

You can and you should use a ruse to misdirect men (e.g. elders) who have no right to the truth (who don't have any right to know that you want to leave the Watchtower), to misdirect anybody who could harm you and your loved ones.

✶ Understanding the Main Points

- What is a ruse?
- What did you learn from Rahab, Gibeonites, Jehu, Joseph, Rebekah, Laban and Leah?
- Which people around you do not have the right to the truth at this time?

✶ Taking My Time to Reflect <Ask 10–100 times>

- What kind of ruse (strategy) can I start using with my JW spouse and family members not to lose them but to win them over, step by step?
- What kind of ruse (strategy) can I start using within the congregation, with the elders and other brothers and sisters?
- What new possibilities will a ruse, strategy etc. create in my life?
- Which approach/decision will create more here?

— ••●•• —

What Is The Danger of Staying Inside?

Briefly: Can you help your JW family more if you leave or if you stay as one of JWs?

What is the danger if you stay inside the Watchtower, if you remain one of JWs?

The Danger of Staying Inside Is Zero If

You know that you are staying inside the Watchtower because of your spouse, because of your family members and loved ones who are still JWs. You can help them much better if you stay as one of JWs.

You know you are able to keep what you really think just to yourself. You are able to resist trying to prove the Watchtower wrong and proving yourself right.

You know that you are using a ruse (e.g. like Rahab) to help your spouse and your loved ones out of the Watchtower. Your conscience is clean because you know exactly what you are doing and why you are doing it.

This way, you can stay within your congregation for as long as needed—before your loved ones are ready to leave with you. It is really only about mastering your feelings which is perfectly possible, as you will see in other parts of this book.

The Danger of Staying Inside Is High If

You feel that you must and have to say publicly what you think and what you believe.

You need to voice your opinions and doubts by commenting against the Watchtower and criticizing its teachings.

You want to show that you are right and the Watchtower is wrong, you want to stir up trouble within the congregation

This way, you won't stay unnoticed and you will be disfellowshipped very soon—before your spouse and family are ready to leave with you! Once disfellowshipped, you won't be able to talk to your loved ones about "spiritual matters" (since they won't be allowed to let you do it) and any opportunities for you to help them will be diminished.

✳ Understanding the Main Points

- Why is there no danger of staying inside the Watchtower with all that you know?
- How can you endanger your position and how can you avoid this?

✳ Taking My Time to Reflect <Ask 10–100 times>

- What possibilities to help my JW family will stay open if I stay as one of JWs?
- What possibilities to help my JW family will close if I leave the Watchtower?
- Which approach/decision will create more here?
- Which approach/decision feels lighter/heavier?
- Which approach/decision feels expanding/limiting?

— ··●·· —

Are You Exiting by Yourself or With Your Loved Ones?

Briefly: What can happen to your relationships once you leave JWs.

If it is only you yourself who wants to get out then your only concerns are probably your own feelings. You can just leave, close the door and start a new life without JWs.

A different approach will be needed if:

Some of your family members are JWs.

You have close friends or coworkers who are JWs.

You are dating or would like to start dating one of JWs.

You have some financial commitments with some JWs (this applies both ways).

✻ Understanding the Main Points

- Can you just leave? Or do you need to wait with your exit for somebody?

✻ Taking My Time to Reflect <Ask 10–100 times>

- What relationships or ties do I have within JWs that will make me weigh my exit strategy more carefully?
- What can I create for my JW family members to make their exit as smooth and as peaceful as possible?
- Which approach/decision will create more here?

— ••●•• —

Why Did You Become One of JWs?

Briefly: Knowing why you became one of JWs will help you leave more easily. The same is true for your JW family members.

It might help you to make it clear to yourself. The best way isn't to look back with regrets but to see things the way they really were.

We cannot change the past. So, the best is to accept the past as an inseparable part of who we are.

At this time, you might not see anything good in the Watchtower. But things are not black and white. Most probably, you must have seen at least some positive things among JWs if you decided to join the organization, i.e. to become a baptized member of JWs.

Maybe you liked being one of JWs because you wanted to be like you parents. You wanted to be in Paradise. You liked the order within the organization. You liked learning to speak publicly at meetings and giving public talks. You liked being with brothers and sisters…

Love Bombing

When you appear at the meeting of JWs for the first time, you are usually given an extremely warm welcome right at the door by an attendant, then by several brothers and sisters. They will be really showing personal interest in you.

You don't see this in most places. Is this really because such true love is displayed only within the true God's Organization? What is behind this affection?

The fact is that this approach is emphasized in the manuals for elders:

> Newly associated ones are especially in need of attention. When they first come to the Kingdom Hall, new ones may feel like strangers; *we want to change that feeling to one of warm friendship*. If you notice a new one standing by himself or talking only with the one who studies with him, take the initiative to approach and greet him and introduce him to others. *Teach attendants to greet new ones, and occasionally remind them to do this… Train all the brothers and sisters to take the initiative in*

approaching new ones and getting acquainted with them…You can associate with new ones at other times also, perhaps visiting with them in their home or yours. *Such personal interest lets them see that genuine love exists among Jehovah's people.* (John 13:35) *It also fills the void created when they cut off former associations and worldly entertainment.* [*Pay Attention to Yourselves and all the Flock*, 1991, p22/23.]

It is also true that many brothers and sisters are genuinely happy to see somebody new coming to the meeting. Most JWs sincerely believe that theirs is the only true religion and they are just happy that somebody else wants to join them.

The result was that you might have felt accepted. It could have been for the very first time in your life. (For example if you never felt this from your parents, classmates, coworkers etc.)

If you felt accepted for the first time in your life, this feeling was extremely strong.

I don't think any JWs involved in the 'love bombing' are really thinking about some 'theocratic war strategies' and are just faking such display of love. Still, the love shown is unusual. It is not feigned but it is sort of artificial. The same way the whole organization of JWs is artificial since it is made up and held together in a top-down, managerial fashion. I am not writing this here to be negative but to be factual, to help you process what is going on.

Once your activity diminishes or you become inactive, such love might disappear. It is good to understand this. Why? Once you are on your way out of the Watchtower, you might not find anything similar anywhere else. Unless you join a similar top-down, high-power group.

So, get ready for that.

The main point of this book is to help you leave JWs together with your loved ones. Please, take your time to think about your JW family members:

What part did the fact that [insert a name of your JW family member] felt accepted play in his/her becoming one of JWs?

How does the answer help you in your next steps?

Fear

If you grew up in a family of JWs you might have heard repeatedly how important it is to "dedicate" yourself to Jehovah as soon as possible and to "get baptized" to display your dedication publicly. A mixture of love bombing and fear might have played a part in all of this. Love bombing was already discussed. So, how about fear? What were or are you afraid of when relating to people outside (in the "world") and inside (members of JWs)?

What part did fear play in your becoming one of JWs?

How was it with your JW family members?

What were you (were they) afraid of?

How does the answer help you in your next steps?

Fear: People Outside (Non JWs)

Please, find some prompts to help you below:

- I was afraid/ashamed to show that I am one of JWs.
- I was afraid/ashamed they would mock me.
- I was afraid I would become like them if I didn't dedicate myself.
- ....

Fear: People Inside (Members of JWs)

Please, find below some prompts to help you.

I am/was afraid that:

- I wouldn't please my parents.
- I wouldn't get life from Jehovah God.
- I wouldn't be good enough for ... (name of the person)
- He/she wouldn't marry me (accept me) if I didn't become one of JWs.
- ....

Why Do You Want to Leave JWs?

What are your reasons to leave the Watchtower?

Try to think about your JW family members, one by one. What reasons could they have not to trust the Watchtower? How can you make use of their doubts?

Please, find below some prompts to help you.

- Failed prophecies and dates for Armageddon.
- Changes in teachings (e.g. generation of 1914, blood).
- Discrepancy between what the organization teaches and what you see in the Bible (e.g. about God, Jesus Christ, organization, governing body, etc.).

16

- Lack of personal freedom and rights to free speech.
- Organization is more important than individuals.
- Pressure to be 'active' in the ministry and to attend repetitive meetings.
- Child sex abuse cases.
- ………

Some leave because they instinctively know something is wrong but they don't know what.

✱ Understanding the Main Points

- What things did you see within the organization that caused you to be interested in becoming one of JWs?
- What practical or good things did you learn while being one of JWs?
- Why do you want to leave JWs?
- What reasons could your JW family members have not to trust the Watchtower?

✱ Taking My Time to Reflect <Ask 10–100 times>

- What possibilities will open to me if I see my past with JWs with no regrets but with appreciation?
- How easy can it be for me to get rid of any fear when it comes to leaving JWs?
- How easy can it be for me not to crave to be accepted by others?
- What possibilities do I have to show (more) acceptance to [insert a name of your JW family member]?
- Which approach/decision will create more here?

— ··●·· —

Choose From Five Exit Strategies

Briefly: Carefully consider which of these five strategies is the best for you and your family in your current situation.

There are five basic exit strategies that aren't necessarily mutually exclusive. These are numbered only for reference purposes. It is up to you to weigh which strategy is the best for you. You can choose to:

1. **Keep a low profile:** "I am in but not very visible."
2. **Be inactive:** "I am in but inactive."
3. **Fade out:** "I am disappearing."
4. **Disassociate yourself:** "I left them."
5. **Get disfellowshipped:** "They kicked me out."

Your choices will depend on several factors:

Where are you yourself now?

Where are your loved ones? (Your spouse, family, children, parents, relatives, friends.)

Where are the people that depend on you?

Where are the people that you depend on?

1/5 Keeping a Low Profile ("I am in but not very visible")

This could be the very best or an extremely good strategy if you have a spouse, family members and/or loved ones who are still active JWs and you don't want to lose them.

How do you keep a low profile? What can you do? These are some options to think about:

You can choose to attend only some meetings or only parts of meetings (e.g. you can arrive right at the start of the public talk and leave right at the end).

You turn in a consistent low monthly report from your ministry. The best is to report a lower time (e.g. 2–5 hours per month) than an absolute minimum required, since you don't want to be considered "weak." This way, you will not attract (much) attention from the elders. And you should report your time regularly, every month. See more in the part on reporting.

You should be very careful with commenting. It might be better to give almost no comments. See more in the part on commenting.

You definitely should not display any doubts and/or any negativity.

If asked by the elders to visit more meetings, you should have a viable ruse (excuse) ready.

2/5 Staying In As an "Inactive" Member ("I am in but inactive")

An "inactive" member is a brother or a sister who has been reporting no time from his or her ministry for several months.

The elders discuss all "weak" and "inactive" members at their meetings. As an "inactive" member, you will be attracting a lot of attention from the elders. They might even assign one or two elders to talk to you with the intent of encouraging you to increase your activity.

Alternatively, they might ask another publisher to be assisting you regularly.

Do you want this sort of attention?

Do you want this sort of assistance?

What can you do about it? What kind of ruse can you use? See some of the tips below:

"Thank you for your help. I completely forgot to report my time from the ministry. I didn't realize what you are telling me now. It is very loving from you. I am sure I can handle this now." (It is important to show that you are not *against* what the elders are telling you.)

"I don't have nearly any time to devote to the ministry. But I witness informally when going to work and back from work or when doing shopping. And I just forgot to report this time from my informal ministry. I will be reporting my time this month. And I will also report time for the previous month(s)." (It is important to send them your report.)

"I will do my best to attend more meetings starting next month." (You don't intend to attend more meetings, but you need to say it. Otherwise the elders will talk about you again. By saying "next month" they have to give you some time to be more active again. In the meantime, they might forget about you.)

"If I can't attend the meeting I always (usually) listen to the meeting online or to the recordings from the meetings." [If you have this possibility in your congregation.]

"Low Profile" vs. Staying In As "Inactive"

What's the difference?

Keeping a Low Profile: You report your time from the ministry each month, but you attend only a few meetings. This way, you don't attract (much) attention from the elders.

Staying In As Inactive: You don't report any time from the ministry, and you attend only a few meetings (e.g. once a month, once in two months). This way, you attract quite a lot of attention from the elders.

3/5 Fading Out ("I am disappearing")

Fade out means to disappear gradually; to vanish gradually. This slower approach is more suitable if you have relationships within JWs that are important for your life.

You will be attending the meetings less and less often; for example, just two meetings a month. And you might come right after the start of the meeting (so that nobody can ask you anything) and leave before the meeting ends or during the meeting (again, so that nobody can ask you anything).

Eventually, you can just appear at one meeting in a month.

If asked, you can use any ruse: You are busy. You don't have much time. You are going through some health issues. And so on.

Start of Fading Out: Attend all the meetings and report e.g. 9 hours per month

After 3 months: attend 6 meetings and report 6 hours per month.

After 6 months: attend 4 meetings and report 4 hours per month.

After 9 months: attend 2 meetings and report 2 hours per month.

After 12 months: attend 1 meeting and report 1 hour per month.
<You present yourself as "active.">

OR

After 12 months: attend 0 meetings and report 0 hours per month.
<You present yourself as "inactive.">

These are just examples. Please, adjust them according to your needs.

Which Meetings to Skip First?

It is a good idea to start skipping the meetings where you would be the most visible. These are meetings with the lowest number of JWs in attendance. With a small number of JWs present, there is the biggest pressure to be visible, to give comments etc. You should avoid this pressure and skip these meetings first.

NOTE: If you stop attending all the meetings and reporting any time from the ministry—you will attract quite a lot of attention from the elders. Please, bear in mind that the congregational elders will be talking about you if you will not be reporting any time from your ministry. They feel it is their responsibility to see that all the brothers and sisters are active in the ministry. Moreover, they will be asked by the Circuit Overseer during his next visit what they had done to help you. Therefore, it might be a much better strategy to use a ruse and report at least 1 hour per month—to avoid the attention of the elders. See more in parts about reporting.

Fading Out by Moving to Another Congregation

The advantage of this move is that the elders in this new congregation do not know you. Thus, they might not be so surprised to see you missing some or many meetings and getting a relatively low service report from you (preferably by SMS, email or through somebody, not personally).

You need to use a viable ruse to make this work. For example, you need to move to a new congregation because:

You have a job that is much closer to this new congregation.

You need to take care of a family member who lives closer to this new congregation.

Fading Out as an Elder or Ministerial Servant

It is much harder to fade out, if you serve in the capacity of an elder or a ministerial servant. It is even much harder if you have been serving as an elder or a ministerial servant for several years. Elders and ministerial servants are *very visible* within the congregations of JWs. However, you don't want to be visible, you want to fade out. Moreover, you need to do all the steps carefully because of your spouse or family members who are still JWs. What can you do?

You can tell the elders that for some time you won't be able to serve in any capacity—e.g. as a Service Overseer or Literature Servant etc.

You have to have a viable excuse ready. For example:

"I have been extremely tired recently."

"They want more and more from me at my workplace and I can't focus on my duties in the congregation."

"I need to take care of my mother/father." <Be careful, since this can be easily verified.>

- After some time, it is a good idea to step down as an elder or ministerial servant. Many brothers and sisters will be surprised. Because of your spouse and family members, you don't want to create any unrest within the congregation. Again, have a viable excuse ready.

4/5 Getting Disfellowshipped ("They kicked me out")

To get disfellowshipped, it is enough to just speak with several brothers and sisters against the Watchtower organization, against the changes in teachings, against their mistakes etc. Sooner or later, you will be reported by some of them to the elders. After that, you will be promptly disfellowshipped. There will be a short announcement to the congregation that you are not one of JWs anymore.

Although the reason for disfellowshipping is never announced, a week or so around the announcement, there's a special talk at one of the meetings. This talk will be given instead of some other part that had been scheduled by the organization. Thus, it will be apparent to everybody that something unusual is happening in the congregation. The topic of this talk will focus on the very reason for your disfellowshipping. Again, nobody will be named. But everybody listening will be able to see why this talk is being delivered. And most brothers and sisters will start avoiding you immediately.

So, weigh your steps to decide if you want to do things this very way.

5/5 Disassociating Yourself ("I left them")

If everything is black and white for you, you can decide just to cut all your ties with JWs from day to day, from minute to minute. You can stop attending any meetings and taking part in any activities with JWs.

There are several approaches to use and to choose from.

You can state to the elders you don't want to be one of JWs anymore.

You can write a farewell letter [or email] to some or all the brothers and sisters that you know, explaining or not explaining your reasons why you don't want to be one of JWs any longer.

Disassociation Letter 1

You can write a letter of disassociation to the elders of your congregation or to the Headquarters of JWs. You don't need to state any reason. It is enough to write something like:

"As of [date], I am disassociating myself from Jehovah's Witnesses. I do not consider myself to be one of Jehovah's Witnesses any longer. Please, delete all my electronic records and send any physical records to my address [state your address]."

Disassociation Letter 2

In case you feel a need to explain more, a good idea is not to use any doctrinal things but an issue that the general public disproves of. Such an issue is for example child sex abuse within JWs.

"As of [date], I am disassociating myself from Jehovah's Witnesses. I can no longer be a part of an organization that is known to cover up child sex abuse. For this reason, I do not consider myself to be one of Jehovah's Witnesses any longer. Please, delete all my electronic records and/or send any physical records to my address [state your address]."

✳ Understanding the Main Points

- What five strategies can you use to leave the organization?
- What advantages and disadvantages are there for you and for your JW family?
- Which strategy have you chosen and how are you going to execute it?

✳ Taking My Time to Reflect <Ask 10–100 times>

- Which of these five strategies will create more: For me, my spouse, my family?
- Which approach/decision feels lighter/heavier?
- Which approach/decision feels expanding/limiting?

— ••●•• —

Should You Report Your Time
From the Ministry?

Briefly: What approach when it comes to reporting is the best for you and your family in your current situation?

If you have a spouse and/or family members who are still JWs you will be in better standing if you report your time from the ministry (even if it is just a "ruse").

Bear in mind:

You need to report your service time monthly (even if it is a "ruse").

Your loved ones must see you as active (even if you do it as a "ruse").

The elders must see you as active—otherwise they will have a hard time explaining what exactly they did to help you to the Circuit Overseer during his visit.

Why Is the Time Reported?

The WT claims that the main purpose of reporting is to know how much literature (magazines, brochures, books etc.) should be printed. And that's why they need the reports from the publishers.

The fact is, that the congregational "literature servant" must keep very exact records of how many pieces of literature (magazines, brochures, books etc.) were ordered by his congregation and how many pieces of literature were left in the congregational stock. These numbers are then sent to the local Branch of JWs from where these are forwarded to a Branch where printing takes place.

Therefore, the only real reason why this reporting is required is to keep constant pressure on the publishers.

All this is just a sort of "activity" game that the organization plays with its members. The organization requires activity, and the members have to report their activity.

Only the "active" members are in good standing; "inactive" or "weak" members are not in good standing.

Now that you understand this game, you can see the pressure the elders in your congregation are under. The elders most probably do not realize these things and so they take all of this very seriously.

If you understand what is going on it will be much easier to make life easier for everybody: for yourself, for your JW family and for the elders.

Just choose to be viewed as a faithful, active JW and report your time from the ministry—even if you don't ever witness to anybody.

By reporting your time each month, you won't attract any unnecessary attention to yourself.

What options do you have?

Minimum time: You can report just a minimum time required per month. This way you will be ranked among the "weak" publishers and you will be attracting a considerable amount of attention from the elders who will be wanting to make you more active in the ministry.

Few hours: You can report a reasonable amount of activity per month. If you report just a few hours, your elders will not grow suspicious.

If you used to turn in a **high report** for many years or months you can choose several approaches to avoid arousing suspicion:

(a) Begin reporting much less time, starting the very next month. It might be a good idea to talk about this openly with one or two elders and tell them that your situation has changed (e.g. because of some health issues) and that your reports will be much lower. By being so open, you will not arouse any suspicion. You should say the same thing to your JW family members (until they are ready to leave together with you). You have to make up some viable excuse. For example, something has changed and you are always extremely tired. The doctors don't know the causes. In case your JW family members or the elders would call your doctor (this might happen in a small town), you need to ask him to be on your side and support you. In fact, the doctor should always keep these matters to himself: "I cannot talk about these matters with anybody else but the patient."

(b) You can start reporting less and less time each subsequent month. Bear in mind that sooner or later some elders will be asking you and will want to know what is happening.

You can decline any offers to go to service with anybody else (even with an elder) by claiming that you witness to people just by yourself when you travel to work and back from work, during breaks at your workplace, during shopping etc. This way, you can report several hours of service every month. If asked, tell the elders this is all you can do and that this makes your relationship with Jehovah God strong. You should have the same explanation ready for your JW family members, in case they ask.

If you decide to attend almost no meetings or just one meeting in a month, send in your report through somebody, by SMS, by email or by any other electronic means.

Send your report on time each month: Don't wait to be reminded by an elder because you will be seen as a problematic publisher. You can set up a reminder to do it, e.g. a recurring monthly reminder on your smartphone or make a mark in your paper calendar/planner etc. This way, you won't be asked any questions and everything will be going smoothly. The elders will be happy—since they will have a report from you. And you will be happy—since you won't be asked any questions.

✷ Understanding the Main Points

- Why is it beneficial for you to be viewed as an "active and faithful" publisher until your spouse and your family members are ready to leave JWs together with you?

✷ Taking My Time to Reflect <Ask 10–100 times>

- How can I make it easy for my spouse and my family to view me as a "faithful and active" member when it comes to my ministry?
- How can I make it easy for the elders?
- Which approach/decision will create more here?

— ••●•• —

Which Meetings to Attend?

Briefly: How you can help your JW family better if you attend (some) meetings.

Attending weekly meetings is a sign of good "spiritual" health for JWs. Therefore, if your meeting attendance suddenly drops to zero you will arouse suspicion—with elders and with your JW spouse and your loved ones as well.

You don't like the meetings anymore—you might even hate them. If so, you should remind yourself why you need to attend the meetings.

You need to **use a ruse** here, again:

> **You attend the meetings because of your JW spouse, because of your JW family members. They need to see you as an active and spiritually healthy member of JWs.**

Tips to Keep a Low Profile at Meetings

Attend at least once a month — your family members and elders should view you as active.

To avoid questions from the elders, arrive during the beginning of the meeting and leave before the final prayer.

If you have to come well before the meeting together with your family, you can spend some time in the bathroom, have a friendly chat with some brothers and sisters, make up some excuse to spend some time in the car and catch up with your family a bit later etc.

Since you will be coming to the meetings primarily because of your spouse and your family members, think how you can show them that you really want to spend time with them.

If possible, sit next to the aisle so that you can leave easily or so that you can go to the bathroom often. Moreover, it is better to sit at the back so as not to be so visible to the speaker.

Alternatively, sit in a corner by a wall in the last row and make use of the time during the meeting to read or study your own materials, e.g. something you need for your work.

Commenting During Meetings

If you were usually quite active with your comments during meetings you will draw the elders' attention if you suddenly stop giving comments altogether.

It is understandable that you don't want to go against your conscience and support with your comments any teaching that you don't believe any more. At the same time, you don't want to arouse any suspicion and you want to be viewed as a faithful member. So what can you do?

Pick a neutral scripture (e.g. from Proverbs, Psalms, Ecclesiastes etc.) from the material studied at the meeting and say something like: "In this context, I really like what is written in the book of Proverbs." And just read that verse.

Do not add any personal viewpoints.

Definitely avoid saying anything negative or anything with double meaning.

Recording the Meetings

Never record any parts of meetings to publish them online, perhaps together with your comments, even if it were under a pseudonym or made-up name. It won't help anybody.

This way, you would be focusing your energy on negative things which won't be good for you.

Sooner or later, it will become known who is behind these recordings.

Memorial: One Meeting Not to Miss?

According to the Watchtower, the Memorial (Lord's Evening Meal) is the only event scripturally commanded to be memorialized by Christians. JWs celebrate the Memorial just once a year, exactly on Nisan 14 (according to the Jewish calendar). Although very few JWs partake of the emblems in the form of unleavened bread and red wine (most probably nobody in your congregation does), for JWs this is the most important meeting in the whole year. They go a long way to invite all their unbelieving relatives, neighbors, friends etc. They conduct special invitation campaigns before that. Most probably, your JW family members will take part in such a campaign. You know all this very well.

Imagine how they would feel if you didn't accompany them to this celebration. They might take it as a clear signal that you are on your way out of the organization. The elders might see it similarly. What to do?

Be present at the Memorial: If you are on the way out and still waiting for your other JW family members to join you, *you should definitely be present* at the Memorial. Be like Rahab. Your JW family members must see you there. Remind yourself how important this occasion is to them. They take it as the most important day in the whole year. You should go out of your way and be at the Memorial together with your JW family members. This is a clear sign for them that you are still one of JWs. Even if the Watchtower's way of the Lord's Supper has lost any meaning for you, it is still extremely important for your JW family members. You can just enjoy being with them. You can even make this day special by preparing a nice dinner for everybody or you can invite your whole family to a restaurant etc. Just show them and let them know how important they are to you and how happy you are to be with them.

You can attend somewhere else: If attending at your Kingdom Hall is absolutely unthinkable for you for some reason, one option could be to attend the Memorial at another Kingdom Hall, e.g. where you are not known so much or where you are unknown. In such a case, you should announce your intentions to your JW family members and really attend this meeting. Alternatively, you can attend it over there together with your JW family members. You should have some good explanation ready for such a decision. Some overzealous elders might even want to verify if you attended the Memorial in that very Kingdom Hall.

Do not partake: Please, do not partake of the emblems in the form of bread and wine. You would draw unnecessary attention to yourself. If you had accepted Jesus Christ as your Lord, you can attend the Lord's Supper at any church in your town or more safely (not to be seen by the other JWs) in some other location. Many Christian churches have the Lord's Supper weekly. Bear in mind that many Christians in the first century C.E. were slaves and they couldn't attend the Lord's Supper if they were told by their master/owner to stay at home and work. If you had accepted Jesus Christ as your Lord, you are safe in Jesus Christ. You don't need to prove it to anybody, let alone to the elders in the congregation of JWs.

Assemblies and Conventions

Assemblies and conventions are something special for most JWs. If your spouse and JW family members feel about them this way, it might be a good opportunity for you to show your loved ones that you are still active and take your faith seriously. A big plus is that dozens, even hundreds of JWs who will be present will see you there. Be like Rahab. You can achieve several good things by attending these assemblies, for example:

- You can support your JW spouse and your family members.

- You can take care of your children (or other family members) during the program so that your spouse can enjoy it more.
- You can take care of the transport and arrange for hotels, which will be appreciated by your spouse.
- You can also socialize and talk to dozens of brothers and sisters who are present.

How to Behave During Assemblies

Since your goal is to leave JWs together with your JW spouse and your family members, you need to wait for them to be ready. Thus, you need to act as a faithful JW during these assemblies.

- Dress and behave appropriately.
- Don't disturb others, although you won't be paying attention to the program. Socialize with other brothers and sisters at places where you will not be disturbing others.
- The attendants shouldn't see you as somebody who didn't come to pay attention to the program; they might report your name to the elders of your congregation.
- Don't talk with anybody about anything against the organization. Bear in mind that first, you need to help your spouse and your family get out of the organization.

Your Last Assembly

What if your JW spouse and family members have already decided to leave the organization together with you? You might still want to attend your last assembly together and use it to talk to others about your decision to leave the WT and reasons for it. Now is the time when you can start helping other JWs get out of the organization, if you want to do it. What to bear in mind?

Printed materials: I have seen some giving out printed materials to brothers and sisters during the assembly. This attracts a lot of attention. Such materials usually end up with attendants in a matter of minutes and you will be shown out. A week after that you will probably be disfellowshipped with no possibility of helping anybody else.

Personal conversations: This is usually a better approach. You need to talk to just one brother or one sister at a time without anybody else listening to your conversation, without any witness of your discussion. This is not because of you, since you are basically already out. This is because of that brother or sister. Only then can that brother or sister be open with you and say what he or she really thinks. Bear in mind that dozens of brothers and sisters will want to meet the one you are just talking with and say at least "hello." Therefore, it might take quite a lot of "small talk" before you will be able to get to your point and say that you are leaving the WT and why. You might have to be very brief. Thus, it could be good to rehearse this part of your conversation. Put yourself into their shoes. Think about what to say and how to say it not to win over that brother or sister with your arguments but to win them over.

Emails: It could be a good idea to follow these conversations with a well-prepared, concise email, which is best to send only after the assembly. These emails should not sound like mass emails, rather, they should be personal.

Arrange to meet: Another approach is not to talk about your decision to leave JWs at the assembly with anybody but to make use of your last assembly just to socialize. You can prepare a shorter list of brothers and sisters with whom you have close relationships and you can offer them to have a cup of coffee together just a few days after the assembly. You can even invite them to your home. Quality could be more than quantity. Bear in mind how long it took you to see through the falsity of the organization and to help your JW spouse and other family members. Bear in mind the family situation of such a brother or sister with whom you want to talk. Do they have a JW spouse or other family members? All these facts could help you adjust your approach so that it is really helpful.

To sum up: Please, consider all the pros and cons, decide what approach would be the most helpful and proceed accordingly.

✻ Understanding the Main Points

- How can you keep a low profile at the meetings and, at the same time, not arouse any suspicion and be viewed as a faithful member?
- How can you show your spouse and your family members that you are here for them and that you really want to spend time with them?
- How about your attendance at the Memorial and at assemblies, including your last assembly?

✻ Taking My Time to Reflect <Ask 10–100 times>

- What possibilities are there for me when it comes to meetings if I don't want to go against my conscience and, at the same time, not arouse any suspicion with my JW spouse, with members of my family and with the elders?

- How can I make the best use of meetings to create more for my family members who are still JWs?
- Which approach will create more?

— ··●·· —

Should You Prove the Watchtower Wrong?

Briefly: Are you more like Raymond Franz or just an ordinary member of JWs?

Many JWs who are leaving the WT have a strong feeling that they *have to* prove the organization wrong. They feel they owe this to themselves, to their family, to their friends, to the world, to all humanity, to God, to the universe.

Firstly, the WT teachings and doctrines have been proven wrong many, many times over. There are publications and websites that detail all the fallacies, misconceptions, manipulations and historical blunders of the WT. It is highly improbable that you will be able to come up with some, or really any new facts.

Secondly, JWs around you might not be open to any of these facts at all. Once you start sharing anything like this with JWs around you, they will have to report you to the elders as somebody with apostate thinking. Moreover, they will do it with the mindset to help you "get back to Jehovah" since this is what they are being taught at the meetings. Proving WT wrong could be quite dangerous if your JW family members are not on your side yet.

Thirdly, bear in mind and carefully consider what all of this will cost you in the process. Please, find below some points to think about and feel free to add some more points of your own.

Just think about this:

Are you more like **Raymond Franz** or just an **ordinary member** of JWs?

Raymond Franz was a member of the governing body of JWs and wrote two books that opened and will continue to open the eyes of thousands. It made sense for him to do what he did.

Please, consider:

What will it cost you (time, emotions, energy, resources) to prove the WT wrong?

Are you able to face the consequences?

Won't you be better off just to help your family members and let it be?

✳ Understanding the Main Points

- How will it help in your own life and in your family if you prove the WT wrong?
- What new facts or a new angle never published before can you bring in?
- If you decide to prove the WT wrong: What is the best time to prove the WT wrong?

✳ Taking My Time to Reflect <Ask 10–100 times>

- What will it create if I prove the WT wrong?
- What will it create (what possibilities will open up) if I give up any need to prove anything and anybody wrong?
- Which approach will create more in my case?

— ••●•• —

Should You Display Your Doubts?

Briefly: How to be careful about displaying your doubts.

Since you decided to read this book, you probably know that the teachings of the Watchtower are false.

However, what consequences will there be if you start displaying your doubts before your JW spouse and family members are ready to leave the WT together with you?

How Some Display Their Doubts

At meetings, they give comments with double meanings or bring up some moot points.

They voice their criticism.

They speak to other brothers and sisters in the congregation about their doubts.

A Better Way

If you want to help your JW spouse and your family get out, you usually won't help them very much by showing your doubts. The effect will most probably be the exact opposite. They will grow suspicious and you might start losing them.

There is a saying:

When in doubt, leave it out.

If you are not sure what effect your words might have, you can just postpone saying them. Yes, it takes patience. However, you are doing it to help your loved ones get out of the WT.

✱ Understanding the Main Points

- How can you endanger your position if you display your doubts to your JW spouse or to your family members?

- How can you make it more difficult to win over your JW spouse or your family members if you display your doubts?
- What will the brothers and sisters in the congregation be compelled to do if you display your doubts to them?

✳ Taking My Time to Reflect <Ask 10–100 times>

- Should I display my doubts and bring up any moot points? Or is it better not to do it?
- What will I create by displaying or by not displaying doubts?
- Which approach will create more in my situation?

— ··●·· —

How to Be Cautious With the Elders in Your Congregation

Briefly: How to use an Open Door approach and be like Rahab with the elders. How to ignore the elders.

It is important to bear in mind that the elders are "serving as overseers" (1Pe 5:2-4) according to the instructions they get from the Watchtower in their special manual for elders and in their special training sessions for elders.

In case they see or even feel anything "apostate," they will follow their instructions to firstly "protect" the organization. You need to be extremely careful and cautious about what you say to any elder and what you say to an elder's wife.

What If the Elders Want to Meet With You

In this case, it depends if only one elder wants to meet with you or if two elders request such a meeting.

One Elder Wants to Meet with You

If only one elder wants to meet with you, he could have been asked to do so by the body of elders or it can be his own initiative. In any case, take this as a warning that the elders have started noticing something about you.

Two Elders Want to Meet with You

If two elders want to meet with you, there are two possibilities:

Shepherding visit: The body of elders has decided that you need a "shepherding visit" and they chose these two elders to do it. The need for a shepherding visit means that the body of elders has started noticing some things about you (lower report, lower meeting attendance etc.). The tone of such a visit will typically be quite friendly, without too many probing questions. They might say something like: "We haven't seen you much recently so we thought it could be a good idea to stop by and see how you are doing."

Two witnesses: The body of elders has decided to send "two witnesses" to investigate and determine your case. The underlying reason is to find out whether a judicial committee needs to be formed. The tone of such a visit will be much less friendly. They might say something like: "A matter has come to our attention that needs to be clarified."

NOTE: Two elders or an elder accompanied by a ministerial servant (aspiring to be an elder) will also have to meet with you if you are a woman at home alone. Only one elder can meet with you if you agree to meet in a coffee shop or in some other public place.

Two Witnesses Principle

The elders will want to apply the principle that there should be two witnesses in the case of any wrongdoing (Deut 19:15; John 8:17). It can be two separate witnesses who can testify to the same act of wrongdoing from the standpoint of the Watchtower (not necessarily two witnesses observing the same act at the same time). Before you respond to any accusation, you need to hear what exactly it is and who said it. In case only one witness heard you saying something against the organization, you can deny it in a way that should make the elders drop the issue.

For example, you can say: "This is a misunderstanding. I didn't say anything like that. The meaning of what I said was…" You can feel pretty safe, as long as you talk with them in a way that assures them everything is OK with you (from the viewpoint of the organization).

How (Not) to Talk With the Elders

Remember Rahab: Use any ruse you can if your goal is to stay within the congregation before your spouse and your family members who are still JWs are ready to leave together with you.

Try to see the situation through the eyes of the elders to better understand what the elders need to hear from you. What picture is acceptable for them? It is sort of OK for elders to see:

That you might be just a bit of a *weaker* member of the congregation, but that you are still *loyal*, and that you definitely pose *no spiritual threat* to anybody.

Be nice with them and, at the same time, be as evasive as possible.

They will want you to speak as much as possible hoping you will really start to speak your mind and reveal something they are after.

Be very careful and cautious about what you say:

Mat 10:16; NWT: "Look! I am sending you out as sheep among wolves; so prove yourselves cautious as serpents and yet innocent as doves."

Remind yourself:

"I am acting like Rahab, now." Use any ruse you can.

"They do not have any right to hear the truth from me, to hear what I really think."

"I will do everything possible to protect myself, my spouse and my family."

"I need to make this meeting as short as possible." Once the meeting becomes uncomfortable for you, you can just use a viable ruse (make some excuse), for example: "I am sorry but just before you came I had a call from my boss and I need to get back to my workplace right now."

Open Door Approach

If you can plan your exit strategy well ahead of time, the "open door approach" can work very well.

Open door approach means telling the elders before they notice anything different about you and before they would start asking you questions.

How to go about it?

You want to report much lower time starting the very next month: Open door approach means that you will talk about this openly with one or two elders and tell them that your situation has changed (e.g. because of some health issues) and that your reports will be much lower. By being so open, you will not arouse any suspicion. You should say the same thing to your JW family members.

You want to start attending fewer meetings: Open door approach means that you will again talk about it with one or two elders.

The best is to talk to two elders at the same time and to make such an interaction short so that the elders don't have time to ask you additional questions. Good timing could be a minute or two before the opening prayer, during the song when you see two elders still in the hallway of the Kingdom Hall etc. You can also give the same information to two elders individually, one by one, on the same day. It is good for you to give these elders two pieces of information at one go:

> "Brothers, I have something to tell you, but it is quite personal. I have started feeling extremely tired recently and I need a lot of rest. My doctor cannot find out what the cause is. The reason I am telling you this is because I won't be able to go to service as much as I used to and as much as I liked. So don't be surprised that **my reports will be much lower**

before my health gets back to normal again. Also, I might have to stay at home and rest instead of going to **some meetings**. I am extremely tired after I come back home from work. Of course, I will be following the meetings online [if you have this possibility] or: I will be listening to the recordings from the meetings. Thank you for your understanding. And please, keep this information to yourselves."

You can be sure that they will not keep it to themselves. They will give it over to the whole body of elders, which is exactly what you want since you won't be asked any questions by the other elders because of your lower report and meeting attendance. This way, you will be able to focus more on helping your JW family members.

The elders will probably call you from time to time to ask if your health is getting better or if you need any help. (They might also ask your other JW family members.) Therefore, it is a good idea to be ready for such a call. Act like Rahab. Be warm and thank them. Tell them that for the time being, your situation has not improved. You can add that you witness informally and that you are glad for the recordings of the meetings (or online meetings). The elders need to feel that although your health has not improved, you are spiritually strong.

This ruse can work for quite a long time, so that you can focus on helping your other JW family members to get out together with you.

Ignoring the Elders

To protect the interests of the Watchtower, the friendly elders can instantly change into merciless interrogators. Meeting with the elders who want to find out about your wrongdoing, e.g. against the organization, can be a harrowing experience.

Are you able to undergo such a meeting?

The solution is simple: You don't have to talk to them! You don't have to let them into your house! If they ring the bell you can just ignore them. You don't have to open the door. You can use an excuse, for example, say you are having a long telephone call. You don't have to tell them when they can come again; when you will have time to talk. You just don't know.

The worst thing that can happen is that they will disfellowship you without any judicial committee. But according to their elders' manual, they would have to have two witnesses of your "wrongdoing."

What if they stop you on the street or ask you in the Kingdom Hall? When in doubt, leave it out. You don't have to say anything you don't want to say or what you could regret, later on. In case you're asked an uncomfortable question, you can keep saying something like: "I don't know what to say at this moment. Let me think about it first." Then avoid them and ignore them.

Bear in mind that the elders really do not have any right or any power to get information from you that you don't want to give them.

✳ Understanding the Main Points

- How will you behave towards the elders in a way that you can help your spouse and your loved ones get out of JWs?
- How can you use to your benefit the open door approach, ruse, ignoring?

✳ Taking My Time to Reflect <Ask 10–100 times>

- How can I be more and more like Rahab when talking with the elders?
- Which approach (open door, ruse, ignoring) will create more in my situation?

— ••●•• —

Dismantling the Authority of the Watchtower

Briefly: Dismantle the authority of the Watchtower, and your family members will leave together with you.

Jehovah's organization, Jehovah's visible organization, God's organization or just *organization*—these terms are everywhere in the Watchtower publications and these are used by Jehovah's Witnesses every day. These terms are a part of the vocabulary of every member.

If you were brought up as one of JWs it became ingrained in you that Jehovah has his special organization.

If you were witnessed to later on in your life, then it's likely that you really started progressing towards baptism as one of JWs only after you accepted with all your heart that Jehovah God has his visible organization on Earth today.

Moreover, you believed that this organization is represented by the *Faithful and Discreet Slave* and by the *Governing Body*. These should be behind all the teachings of the organization and behind the *new light,* they should be guiding members to be active witnesses for Jehovah God.

Leaving Because of Doctrinal Differences

There are JWs who leave the organization for all kinds of reasons, for example: Changes in the teachings of the Watchtower during the years (e.g. on blood, generation of 1914, Armageddon etc.). Extreme control over the lives of the members (the WT has binding suggestions to almost all areas of life). Doctrinal issues (Jesus Christ, heaven, eternal life etc.) Cases of covered sexual abuse.

It is a good situation if you are able to come to an agreement on any of these points with your JW spouse and family members and then leave the organization together based on any of these points.

I know a huge number of former JWs who have left the organization and, even after many years, they still do not believe in the Trinity (as an example; which doesn't mean that you should).

NOTE: Raymond Franz, the former member of the governing body and the author of the *Crisis of the Conscience* also never believed in the Trinity, as I learned from him personally.

However, not a single one of them has the slightest doubts that the teaching about the authority of "governing body" and the "faithful and discreet slave" is totally made up. Each one of these former JWs is 100% clear that the Watchtower has no authority at all.

That's why this book does not focus on proving doctrinal matters but concentrates on downplaying and destroying the role of the organization.

Taking Away the Role of the Organization

The term Jehovah's organization is definitely full of meaning for one of JWs. One cannot be a real witness of Jehovah without actually believing in His organization.

That's why diminishing, downplaying or downright disputing the authority of Jehovah's organization usually leads to judicial cases. The elders will deal with such an offending member with more severity than in any other cases, such as immorality, lying, stealing etc. Such a member will be categorized as a very dangerous person and will typically be disfellowshipped.

Be careful: If your spouse, your family members and your loved ones are still fully JWs—be extremely careful about how you speak about Jehovah's organization, the Faithful and Discreet Slave, and the Governing Body.

A better way: To help your spouse, your JW family members and your loved ones—they have to first see that God *does not use* any governing body and any organization like this.

A much better way is to elicit their own negative comments and then decide what to say and what not to say.

What might also work are open-ended questions, such as: "How do you feel about this (new) piece of information in the last Watchtower?"

The best approach is, probably, to show them that there was no centralized authority in the Bible (no "governing body") in the first century—neither in Jerusalem, nor anywhere else. This can be seen if you read the account in the books of Acts carefully. You can read and discuss this account with your JW loved ones together. The main points are in Acts 9-15.

See the step by step procedure in the Appendix, under the heading "No Governing Body or Central Authority In the Bible."

✻ Understanding the Main Points

- How can you see for yourself that God never used any centralized authority, or governing body in the New Testament?
- How can you show it to somebody else?

✻ Taking My Time to Reflect <Ask 10–100 times>

- What possibilities do I have to show my JW spouse and my family members that God never used any centralized authority (governing body)?
- How can I do it in the most loving way to win them over?
- Which approach will create more here?

— ··●·· —

How Chronological Bible Reading Can Help Your Family

Briefly: How chronological Bible reading changes the mindset and helps to see there was no "governing body" in the first century C.E.

By reading the Bible together with your JW spouse and with your family members, you can help them see *for themselves* that the teachings of the WT are false. This is probably the most natural way to help them see that there was no "governing body" that directed the congregations in the first century C.E.

If you are *not* in the habit of reading the Bible together with your spouse and with your family, introduce it step by step. For example, when considering the scripture from *Examining the Scriptures Daily,* read the larger context *together* or even the whole chapter from the Bible.

Read the Bible Together Chronologically

This is your goal—to progress to reading the Bible in a chronological way together.

Why? When you finally get to reading the book of Acts chronologically, it is quite apparent that apostle Paul didn't do anything under any supervision of any centralized authority ("governing body"). It is quite clear that there was nothing like a "governing body" in Jerusalem or anywhere else.

So, just from reading the book of Acts and Paul's apostolic letters, your loved ones will see that no "governing body" existed in the first century. This way, their trust in the organization will crumble. Moreover, they will be open to more direct communication and will be ready to learn more, and eventually get out of the organization together with you.

That's why you first need to show them the beauty of reading the Bible chronologically and reading the same story (e.g. from Jesus' life) as it was described by different writers.

Let us have an example about the last Passover that Jesus celebrated.

Matthew 26:17-19 describes it quite briefly, saying that Jesus sent his disciples to get things ready. Mark 14:12-16 adds that Jesus sent *two* of his disciples. And Luke 22:7-13 completes the narrative with their names, Peter and John, and adds more details.

Changing the Mindset

Jehovah's Witnesses are taught they need help to really understand the Bible:

> "It is unlikely that someone who simply reads the Bible without taking advantage of divinely provided aids could discern the light. That is why Jehovah God has provided 'the faithful and discreet slave,' foretold at Matthew 24:45–47. Today that 'slave' is represented by the Governing Body of Jehovah's Witnesses." [w92 5/1, p.31]

Pattern Interrupt: Thus, reading the Bible *chronologically* is a very new concept for one of JWs. It can work wonders as a pattern interrupt—it interrupts the old pattern to make room for new ways of thinking. The benefits are exactly what you are looking for in your JW spouse and your family members. For example, they will start to realize that two adjacent verses could describe events happening many years apart, at places hundreds of miles away from each other, without our modern-day means of fast, comfortable transportation and without our modern-day means of effective communication (such as telephones and internet).

Hopefully, they will start to:

- **Open their minds:** Gradually they will be opening to new things.

- **See things in a new way:** They will start to see facts that they have never noticed before and connect facts in completely new ways.

- **View things independently:** Till now they were dependent on the explanations from the Watchtower, not they will be independent.

You can achieve all of this step by step just by reading the Bible chronologically, starting from the New Testament.

How to Read the Bible Chronologically

Which facts should we look for when reading the Bible chronologically? We should look at least for these facts:

- **Time:** What time elapsed between two adjacent verses? What time elapsed between Acts 9:25 and Acts 9:26 if we use the cross-reference in NWT (Ga 1:17-18)? The three full years elapsed before apostle Paul went from Damascus to Jerusalem "to visit Cephas" and "saw no one else of the apostles, only James the brother of the Lord." It took three full years after his conversion, before Paul went to Jerusalem!

- **Place:** Which places are mentioned in the passages? In our example, it is Damascus and Jerusalem.
- **Distance:** What is the distance between Damascus and Jerusalem? Using today's data, by plane, it is 218 kilometers (136 miles). By car, it is 2976 kilometers (1849 miles). In the first century, the distance was most probably longer, due to much less developed roads. If you could travel 15 miles a day in the first century, you would need 123 days (i.e. four months) to travel from Damascus to Jerusalem, without one single day of rest during such a journey.

This way, you can start seeing the Bible narrative in a completely different way.

What you will need:

- Chronological Bible and Bible with cross-references (e.g. *NWT: The New World Translation*). It is a very powerful thing to use the cross-references from the very *New World Translation*.
- A good map of Bible lands, with Paul's missionary trips.

First, you need to get a good chronological Bible for yourself and start reading it.

Chronological Bible

There are all kinds of "chronological" Bibles but not all of them are made in a similar way. After trying most of them, from my own experience and from the experience of others whom I was helping, I can fully recommend:

The Reese Chronological Study Bible: King James Version

It features dating similar to what JWs use (e.g. the date of creation is set to 4004 B.C.E.; JWs use 4026 B.C.E.).

The chronology in the Book of Acts is the closest to what you need to show that there was no centralized authority ("governing body") in the first century C.E., if you will be using the approach from the Appendix in this book ("No Governing Body or Central Authority In the Bible").

The text in the *Reese Bible* appears in the following sequence in the book of   Acts: Ac 1:1–**9:22; Ga 1:17; Ac 9:23-28; Ga 1:18;** Ac 9:29-43; Ac 10:1–12:23; James 1:1-5:20; Ac 12:24-15:12; Ga 2:7-10; Ac 15:13-35; Ga 2:11-14; Ac 15:34-18:17; 1 Thes 1 etc. (The parts in bold are the most important for our purposes.)

The other options are some modern translations listed below. However, these are not as detailed in the book of Acts as the *The Reese Chronological Study Bible.*

The One Year Chronological Bible NIV (NKJV, NLT)

> The text in the *The One Year Chronological Bible (NIV, NKJV, NLT)* appears in the following sequence in the book of Acts (at least in the editions that I have):
>
> Ac 1:1-14:28; Ga 1:1-6:18; Ac 15:1-18:3; 1 Thes 1 etc. Thus, there are fewer details.

If you want to be 100% sure about getting the correct title, you can use a link to these Bibles from the website: www.FreeFlowPal.com

Note: When you make a purchase from links on this website, I may earn a small commission.

In this case, it is better to get a physical Bible, a real book, not an eBook, since you will want to read this Bible together with your JW spouse and family members. You want to have this Bible open on the table, mark or highlight certain passages and get back to them easily etc.

Chronological Bible Reading Plan: If you cannot afford a physical chronological Bible or you just don't want to buy it for any reason, you can use a chronological Bible reading plan—print it out and follow it together with your spouse and family members.

Again, there are many chronological reading plans. After trying most of them, I selected a plan that is the closest to our purposes of dismantling the claims about any centralized authority ("governing body").

You can download the best free Chronological Bible Reading Plan from the website: www.FreeFlowPal.com

Try this reading plan on your own first. You will see that this approach is not very "user-friendly" as you will have to flip between pages all the time. Also, bear in mind that people subconsciously tend to put more trust into a solid, printed book than a PDF reading plan downloaded from the internet. These are just points to consider; the final decision whether to use a printed plan or a chronological Bible is totally up to you.

I knew that our family would not welcome a printed reading plan. Therefore, I used two chronological Bibles: *The One Year Chronological Bible NIV* when we started in the New Testament and *The Reese Chronological Study Bible: King James Version* when we started reading the book of Acts.

How to Start With a Chronological Bible

It is not advisable to begin reading the Bible chronologically starting with Acts, chapter 9. Most probably, you would scare your spouse and your family members away and lose them in the process. Therefore, you need to start gradually and motivate them. You can take some ideas from the Preface of *The One Year Chronological Bible NIV*:

"Have you ever wondered when an event in Scripture occurred? Have you ever puzzled over the order of biblical events or how much time passed between those events? Have you struggled just to read through the Bible? A Bible that is easy to read and will help you understand the flow of the biblical story is what you need.

The One Year Chronological Bible contains the entire text of the New International Version, arranged in the order the events actually occurred. This unique viewpoint allows you to read the whole Bible as a single story and to see the unfolding of God's plan in history.

Reading the Bible in chronological order will help you gain a unique perspective on Scripture that you could not get from reading a regular Bible cover to cover.

For example, after you read about the time David escaped the soldiers who were sent to capture him in 1 Samuel 19:1-17, you will immediately read in how David poured out his heart to God in response to this situation in Psalm 59.

When you read the letters of Paul, you will see how they fit into the framework of his missionary journeys recorded in the book of Acts. You will be able to see how various passages fit together into a single, unfolding story…

You will also be able to place events on a timeline much more accurately, thus visualizing them better and appreciating them more."

What to Stress to Your Family

First, get your own Chronological Bible and get acquainted with it.

Then, sit down with your family, show and motivate them: Read from it together, starting in the New Testament. Be enthusiastic about the benefits. Suggest that you can read together like this every day, only one or two pages for example. After all, JWs were formerly called the Bible Students, right?

The point is to get into an everyday habit of reading the Bible this way together, starting from the New Testament. It is important to do it this way for several weeks before you get to the book of Acts. Step by step, your family members will develop a new way of thinking:

They will start to think about the events within the context.

Since you don't want them to go around and announce to others that you read the Bible chronologically at home, it might be a good idea to put this Bible into some cover so that the term "Chronological" is not seen all the time. You will be reading the Bible chronologically together every day but they don't need to be reminded of this term so much.

✳ Understanding the Main Points

- What are the advantages of chronological Bible reading?
- Which chronological Bible will be the best for your family?

✳ Taking My Time to Reflect <Ask 10–100 times>

- What possibilities do I have to introduce the reading of the chronological Bible to my spouse and/or family members in such a way that they will be excited for it?
- What occasion or timing would be the best to introduce them to chronological Bible reading?
- Which approach will create more here?

— ••●•• —

Protecting Your Family and Marriage

Briefly: How to use a ruse within your marriage to be viewed as a faithful member until your spouse is ready to leave together with you.

Leaving a manipulative group, sect, cult or a religion ranks among extremely stressful situations that might exact a high toll on one's marriage.

If only one spouse leaves JWs and the other one stays in, the marriage might be endangered. JWs are taught in their literature that living in the same household with an apostate (former JW) can seriously endanger their spirituality.

Don't Become an Apostate in Your Family

"Disfellowshipped and disassociated ones are shunned by those who wish to have a good relationship with Jehovah... We need to be especially cautious about contact with disfellowshipped persons who have apostatized." [ks91, p. 103]

The Watchtower publications suggest, quite clearly, how family members should treat an "apostate" in their midst:

"Display Christian Loyalty When a Relative Is Disfellowshipped. In the Immediate Household: The Watchtower of September 15, 1981, page 28, points out regarding the disfellowshipped or disassociated person: 'Former spiritual ties have been completely severed. This is true even with respect to his relatives, including those within his immediate family circle. . . . That will mean changes in the spiritual fellowship that may have existed in the home. For example, if the husband is disfellowshipped, his wife and children will not be comfortable with him conducting a family Bible study or leading in Bible reading and prayer. If he wants to say a prayer, such as at mealtime, he has a right to do so in his own home. But they can silently offer their own prayers to God. (Prov. 28:9; Ps. 119:145, 146) What if a disfellowshipped person in the home wants to be present when the family reads the Bible together or has a Bible study? The others might let him be present to listen if he will not try to teach them or share his religious ideas.'" [km 8/02 pp. 3-4]

Your spouse and/or your family members will want to heed this advice. That's why you don't want to put yourself into a situation where they would view you as an apostate and as a threat to their spiritual well-being.

Do everything in your power to leave the organization together with your spouse, together with all the members of your family. This calls for a very patient strategy on your part.

Spend More Time Together

Act like Rahab. Continue reporting several hours a month from your ministry (even if you don't take part in it at all) and attend at least some meeting each month to maintain the look of a faithful (although a "weaker") member. Do all this not to arouse any suspicion on the part of your JW spouse and your family members.

You can also make good use of the suggestions from the Watchtower to spend more time together as a family. For example:

> "Families likewise need time to relax... If families play together, they are more likely to stay together!" [w93 9/1 pp. 15-20]

It is extremely important for you to start strengthening the bonds with your spouse, with your children and with all the members of your family right now. Exiting JWs is a stressful situation and your family needs to be as strong as possible to emerge from this situation victorious.

✳ Understanding the Main Points

- How will your JW spouse and family members have to behave towards you once you disassociate yourself or once you are disfellowshipped?

- How can this put a big strain on the relationship with your spouse and with other family members?

- How can you spend more time together with your spouse and with your family members?

✳ Taking My Time to Reflect <Ask 10–100 times>

- What can I do not to be viewed as an apostate by my JW spouse and my family members?

- What can I do to be viewed as a faithful JW by my spouse and my family members before they are ready to leave the Watchtower?

— ••●•• —

Protecting Your Children

Briefly: Keep putting off the baptism of your children until they are ready to leave JWs together with you.

The Watchtower uses a very sly approach with children. On one hand, they claim that it is a highly responsible step to get baptized, on the other hand, they are happy to baptize children as young as 10 years old, or even younger.

The Watchtower typically points to these examples from the New Testament:

Timothy (2 Tim 3:14, 15). But the Bible doesn't show at what age he was baptized.

Jailer from Philippi who got baptized with his family (Acts 16:25-33). The Bible doesn't say that there were any children baptized.

Philip's four daughters (Acts 21:8, 9). Again, no age is mentioned in the Bible.

None of these examples can really be taken as a motivation to get baptized before you are an adult.

The Watchtower typically points to these examples from the Old Testament:

Joseph was about 17 years old when he was sold to slavery by his brothers. (Gen. 37:2; 39:1-3). Sad as it was, this event has nothing to do with baptism at a young age.

Young **Samuel** "was ministering before Jehovah ... though he was just a boy" (1 Sam. 1:24-28; 2:18-20). Again, this has nothing to do with baptism. For example, a child can help a literature servant without being baptized.

Josiah was eight years old when he became king (2 Chron. 34:1-3). Again, this has nothing to do with baptism.

The important thing is: Children typically do not want to rush into baptism. However, once your child is baptized as one of JWs, the same principles will apply to him or her as to any other Jehovah's Witnesses:

In case you get disfellowshipped or you disassociate yourself, your child should not talk with you about any spiritual matters. The doors will be closed.

What can you do?

Try to Postpone Their Baptism

What can you say?

"Dedication and baptism are very important steps."

"It could be best to wait till you are a grown-up."

"Put your baptism off till the next (special) assembly." In the meantime, get as close to your child as possible.

What else can you do to put off their baptism?

Encourage your children to spend time with your unbelieving relatives: with their cousins who are not JWs etc.

Invite your children's "worldly" classmates to your home.

Encourage your children to spend time with these "worldly" classmates, supposedly to "witness" to them by your behavior.

What can you do if you are under 18 years of age and reading this book?

Do everything possible to put off your baptism.

You can keep repeating: "Baptism is a very serious step. I still need some time for that."

✳ Understanding the Main Points

- How can you help your children to postpone their baptism?
- Who else can help your children postpone their baptism?

✳ Taking My Time to Reflect <Ask 10–100 times>

- What possibilities do I have to get closer to my children and to spend more time with them?

— ··●·· —

Avoiding Divorce and Separation

Briefly: Use a ruse not to be viewed as a "spiritual danger" by your spouse before he/she is ready to leave JWs together with you.

According to the Watchtower "the only divorce ground that actually severs the marriage bond is *porneia* (sexual immorality) on the part of one's marriage mate. The follower of Christ may avail himself of that divorce provision if that is his desire, and such a divorce would free him to marry an eligible Christian.—1Co 7:39." [it-1 pp. 639-643; *Divorce*]

Separation Because of Endangered Spiritual Life

However, the Watchtower also speaks about "legal separation" after which a Christian is not free to pursue a third party with the intention of remarrying. The term "legal separation" is basically a euphemism for a divorce after which the "innocent JW" cannot remarry (until the former marriage partner has sexual relations with his/her new partner after this break-up).

The reason for such "legal separation" can also be "if matters reach the point where spiritual life is endangered." Thus, if your JW spouse feels that his/her "spiritual life is endangered," they might seek "legal separation," since this way they will "obey God as ruler rather than men." What will the result be? Your marriage will fall apart because of spiritual differences. Moreover, the break-up will be sanctioned by the Watchtower:

> "Are there situations that may justify separation or possibly divorce from a marriage mate even if that one has not committed fornication? Yes, but in such a case, a Christian is not free to pursue a third party with a view to remarriage... If a spouse constantly tries to force a marriage mate to break God's commands in some way, the threatened mate may also consider separation, *especially if matters reach the point where spiritual life is endangered*. The partner at risk may conclude that the only way to "obey God as ruler rather than men" is to obtain a legal separation.—Acts 5:29." [*fy* chap. 13 pp. 153-162; *If Marriage Is at the Breaking Point*]

To paint a complete picture, there are two more reasons that the Watchtower gives for "legal separation": willful (financial) nonsupport and extreme physical abuse.

This is extremely important to bear in mind. Your spouse might feel pressed to act according to what is published in the Watchtower literature, in the case that the "spiritual life is endangered."

If you want to keep your marriage intact, there's no reason to hurry things up and to push your JW spouse to get out of the Watchtower before he/she is ready to leave.

Did You Go Too Far?

What can you do if you went too far and your spouse started viewing you as an "apostate" and as a "spiritual danger"? I am not a marriage counselor. Still, I can give you some tips here that I know worked while I was helping hundreds of JWs getting out. The entries in this list aren't in any specific order. You need to consider these options based on your own situation:

Talk, talk, talk. Open communication might help a lot.

Apologize repeatedly and sincerely.

Offer to read the Bible together (you can use the Chronological Bible).

Rekindle your love. Look at the photos where you are together. Suggest a holiday together. Spend a weekend together.

Go to a place where you first met or where you experienced something memorable together.

Ask: "Why should any teaching be more important than our marriage? Some teachings have been changed. What if this teaching changes in a year or two?"

Offer to read the books by Raymond Franz, the former member of the governing body of JWs. ("If what you believe is the truth, you don't have to be afraid of anything, let alone some book. Please, read it because of our marriage.")

Which friend(s) can help? Who can talk to your spouse? It can be one of JWs or a non-JW friend (e.g. a wise aunt, parents, colleague etc.).

Could a marriage counselor help?

At worst, offer to live separately for some time (e.g. for a week or two). You might see things differently after that.

✱ Understanding the Main Points

- What can you do to postpone separation and divorce?
- Who can you ask for help?

56

✱ Taking My Time to Reflect <Ask 10–100 times>

- What can I do to rekindle our communication and love?
- What possibilities do I have to open the lines of communication?
- Which approach will create more here?

— ••●•• —

How You Can Be Safer If You Stay an Interested Person

Briefly: Keep putting off your baptism to stay an interested person; you will be able to help your JW family much better in this position.

If you were brought up in a family of JWs it is expected that you will become an official member—that you will get baptized as one of JWs. However, baptism as one of JWs is an irreversible step. Once you get baptized as one of JWs there are only two ways out:

You can disassociate yourself.

You can get disfellowshipped.

Both of these things mean that you will become an "apostate" and that you will be shunned by JWs.

However, as long as you stay an interested person, your position is totally different and much better. You will be viewed positively—as a prospective member.

✱ Understanding the Main Points

- What are the advantages of staying just an interested person?
- How can I postpone my baptism?

✱ Taking My Time to Reflect <Ask 10–100 times>

- What possibilities are open to me if I stay just an interested person?
- What possibilities do I have to help my JW spouse and our family members if I stay just an interested person?
- Which approach will create more here?

— ··●·· —

Giving Up Your Investment

Briefly: Count your losses; it calls for a lot of strength to admit how much you have wasted with JWs.

The longer you have been one of JWs the more difficult it seems to leave. Why is that? Consciously or subconsciously, you feel how much you have put into your faith—time, emotions, resources, money... You feel the severity of how many other things you have given up to be one of JWs.

Personally, I was one of JWs for 25 years, most of those serving as an elder and a pioneer. If I count just the meeting attendance and public ministry, I have given over 20,000 hours to the WT. All this time could have been spent somewhere else. In addition to that, there were other activities, monetary contributions etc.

And now, after all those years, I had to say to myself: "This was a bad investment."

This is a very sobering experience, which calls for a lot of strength. It is not easy to admit to yourself that so much time and so many resources were wasted with this religion. And you might have also wasted the time and resources of your spouse, family members and others—if they were "helping" you to become one of JWs or if you were "helping" them.

Nevertheless, it is important to be honest about it, to accept these facts and move on.

Your Spouse, Family Members and the Investment

Is your spouse ready to see things the same way you do? How about your other family members?

A highly committed JW won't want to own up to the fact that the time and resources they put into the organization should suddenly become void. They might need a lot of time to acknowledge these facts.

I know several Jehovah's Witnesses who chose to patiently stay in the congregation, keep a low profile, and wait for their beloved spouse to become aware of the facts for 3, 5, 8, 10 years and even longer!

I know a dear brother who was waiting patiently like this for almost 15 years, keeping a low profile within the congregation. When I asked him if it was a worthwhile effort, he said: "I love my dear wife, I love my children and grandchildren—they are all Jehovah's Witnesses. If I left the organization 15 years ago, I might have stayed with my wife, but our relationship wouldn't be the same. I couldn't have the same relationship with my grandchildren. Who knows if I would be even allowed to see them? So for me it was definitely worth the wait."

On the other hand, I know a brother who left the organization more than 10 years ago, loudly voicing his disapproval of JWs teachings. The result? He did stay with his JW wife. However, he can only see his grandchildren in photos.

✳ Understanding the Main Points

- Where did you make a bad investment when it comes to JWs?
- To what extent are your family members ready to accept that they made a bad investment with the Watchtower?
- What do you need to forgive in this respect?

✳ Taking My Time to Reflect <Ask 10–100 times>

- How can I best accept that my investment with JWs (my time, emotions, resources, money) was a bad one?
- What possibilities will open up to me if I forgive?
- How can I best help my spouse and family members to see and accept that they made a bad investment with the Watchtower?
- What would be the best timing to share these ideas with them?
- Which approach will create more here?

— ••●•• —

Protecting Your Identity Online

Briefly: Don't compromise your exit strategy with your JW family by reckless use of online resources.

Again, I cannot stress enough that this part is written for somebody who is leaving the WT and waiting for his JW spouse and family members to leave together with him. You shouldn't be viewed as an "apostate" before they are ready to leave together with you.

Some exiting brothers and sisters feel a need to visit websites, online forums, Facebook groups etc. where all kinds of things (mostly negative) are shared about JWs.

Some even feel that they have to share their experiences with the world.

If this is what you need to do, then it is a good idea not to do it under your real name—if you don't want to arouse any suspicion on the part of your JW spouse, family members and elders.

Please, consider using some of these approaches:

Make another (Facebook) profile for this purpose, with a pseudonym. Log-off at the end of each session.

Don't "like" any posts.

Use a new, dedicated email address for this purpose.

If you really need to share your thoughts anywhere online, write in a different way than you normally do.

Don't share any pictures of yourself or brothers and sisters from your congregation.

Don't share any recordings from your congregation (audio, video).

Use your own computer for these online activities, a computer nobody else uses.

The safest thing could be to read these online materials on your own smartphone. If you do, never give your smartphone to anybody; never let your children play with it.

If you really need to use a shared, family computer for your online activities, you should learn:

Not to store any of your passwords in that computer.

Use an anonymous web browser (e.g. Tor Browser).

Use a VPN to allow anonymous surfing and to change your IP address.

If you have read the two books by Raymond Franz, the late former disfellowshipped member of the governing body, you already have most of the facts that you will ever need:

Crisis of Conscience by Raymond Franz

In Search of Christian Freedom by Raymond Franz

These are big books. It might not be so easy to hide them from the eyes of your spouse and family members before they are ready to read them. So, it might be a better idea to have and read these books in an electronic format, as eBooks, and read them on a device that you never share with anybody else (e.g. on your own smartphone).

Have an Alibi Ready

If your spouse, family member or somebody from your congregations catches you viewing "apostate" materials online, you have to have a viable excuse ready. Something like this could work:

> "Recently, I have been confronted about my beliefs at work and I found it difficult to respond. I thought that it would help me to have a look at some of these websites to see these questions and get ready for them. I can see now how unreasonable this approach is."

Don't Be an Activist

If your spouse and family members are not ready to leave together with you, yet, it might not make much sense for you to help others get out. First and foremost, you should take care of your family. Only after your own family is safely out, you can start thinking about helping others.

✱ Understanding the Main Points

- How can you behave online so as not to compromise yourself?
- How can you read books to hide them from the eyes of your spouse and family members before they are ready to read them?
- What alibi can you have ready?

✱ Taking My Time to Reflect <Ask 10–100 times>

- How much more peace of mind can I have if I completely avoid any online forums, Facebook groups etc. aimed at JWs?
- How much time, energy and resources can I save by avoiding things related to the WT?
- Which approach will create more here?

— ••●•• —

Preparing to Live With the Consequences of Shunning

Briefly: Be prepared that you won't even be greeted by your (former) brothers and sisters.

If you know that you will be disfellowshipped or if you plan on disassociating yourself, get ready for shunning. Your (former) JW brothers and sisters will have to avoid you, they won't even respond to your greeting, since they have to do as told by the Watchtower.

Prepare for that. Make new friends long before you lose any possibility of contact with your (former) brothers and sisters from the congregation.

✻ Understanding the Main Points

- How will your (former) JW brothers and sisters treat you once you are disfellowshipped or after you disassociate yourself?

✻ Taking My Time to Reflect <Ask 10–100 times>

- How can I prepare for the fact that I will be shunned?
- How can I not take it personally?
- Which approach will create more here?

— ••●•• —

In Front Of a Judicial Committee

Briefly: Be like Rahab with the elders, use a ruse and show that you are repentant. You will be in a better position to help your family get out if you stay as one of JWs.

A judicial committee is formed if the accusation has substance and if the offense is serious enough to result in disfellowshipping:

> "Before forming a committee, elders determine if the accusation has substance. It must Scripturally be an offense serious enough to result in disfellowshipping. There must either be two witnesses or a confession of wrongdoing. If there is not enough evidence to form a committee but serious questions have been raised, two elders may be assigned to investigate the matter." [ks91, p. 109]

If the committee for example finds out that you have truly spoken against the faithful and discreet slave, the next thing they will want to see is if there is sincere repentance on your part or lack of it. How can true repentance be recognized, according to the book for elders?

> "Has the individual contritely prayed to Jehovah and sought His forgiveness and mercy?
> Caution. Some wrongdoers, though repentant, find it difficult to pray. Has he admitted his wrongdoing, either voluntarily to some of the elders before the hearing or when confronted by his accusers?
> Caution: Some people are so deeply ashamed that they are reluctant to speak. Or they have difficulty expressing themselves.
> Does he have deep regret over a damaged relationship with Jehovah, remorse over the reproach he has brought upon Jehovah's name and people, and sincere longing to come back into God's favor?"

Therefore, if you don't want to be disfellowshipped and leave the organization before your JW spouse and family members are ready to leave with you, you need to do this one thing:

Show That You Are Repentant

You need to show that you are repentant! You need to show that you deeply regret what happened!

Moreover, you need to show it and display your repentance to elders even if you think otherwise.

You need to say something like this:

"I have prayed about this to Jehovah many times and asked for His forgiveness and mercy. I have even prayed in tears."

It will be a ruse. You will be acting like Rahab, again. But the elders do not have any right to hear the truth from you. They do not have any right to tear your family apart. Bear in mind that you are doing all this just to stay in the congregation until your spouse and your family members are ready to leave together with you. You know that you can help them better as long as you are viewed as a "faithful" member.

✳ Understanding the Main Points

- What one thing will the elders want to see from you?

✳ Taking My Time to Reflect <Ask 10–100 times>

- How easy can it be for me to show my repentance to elders to stay in good standing because of my spouse and my family until they are ready to leave JWs together with me?
- How easy can it be for me to act like Rahab with the elders?
- How easy can it be for me to keep my peace under these circumstances?
- Which approach will create more here?

— ··●·· —

How to Mitigate the Exit Effects

Briefly: How to mitigate the effects of your exit by planning your exit well.

It is good to bear in mind what can happen once a JW member leaves the congregation of Jehovah's Witnesses. Let's have a long-time member who was extremely zealous, comes from a JW family and works with other JWs in his/her workplace. Let's see some possible effects of leaving JWs.

A leaving JW might:

- lose all his JW friends and his social circle,
- lose contact with his JW family members,
- lose his marital partner (in case of divorce or separation because of "spiritual danger"),
- lose his parents, siblings, children, grandchildren, relatives (because of "spiritual danger"),
- lose regular activities (meetings, service),
- lose job opportunities (JWs are allowed to employ an "apostate" but they might try to get rid of such worker),
- lose income (after losing a job with a JWs company).

This list is an extreme example. With good planning and timing, most of these things might never occur. Nevertheless, it is very important to be aware of these facts.

✳ Understanding the Main Points

- What exit effects can you expect in your case, once you leave JWs?

✳ Taking My Time to Reflect <Ask 10–100 times>

- How can I mitigate the exit effects as much as possible?
- Which approaches from this book will create more for me?

— ••●•• —

How to Make New Friends

Briefly: How to start building your support network, before you leave JWs together with your family.

If you have been very serious with JWs you were most likely avoiding contact with the world outside the Watchtower since you believed that all these associations are "unwholesome" for your spiritual well-being. Even at your workplace, you might have not really made any real friends; you just knew them as your co-workers. Moreover, if you work in a company managed by JWs then your world might have consisted of JWs only.

Before you leave JWs for good, you want to have your spouse and your family members with you. Even in that case, you will need new friends. Therefore, it is a good idea for you to start building new friendships as soon as possible and do it in such a way that you don't arouse suspicion.

As you start fading away or start being much less active within your congregation of JWs you will see that your brothers and sisters will not want to be with you as they used to be; they will just see you as much less active and they will perceive this as a threat to their own spiritual well-being. You will start losing close friends within your congregation. Therefore, it is a wise thing to start making new friends—long before you leave JWs for good (ideally together with your spouse and with all your family members).

Some tips include:

Start getting closer with your non-JW siblings (physical brothers and/or sisters) and with your non-JW relatives if you have any (parents, grandparents, children, grandchildren, cousins, uncles, aunts etc.).

Start getting closer with your current or former classmates. Look for and take part in your school/class reunion meetings. Join your class and/or school Facebook group. Actively meet your current or former classmates.

Start making friends at your workplace. Get to know your coworkers as much as you can.

Start making friends among your neighbors. Go shopping with them. Invite them over to your house.

Start going to a gym, aerobic or yoga workouts etc. Join a club with activities that are viewed "neutral" by JWs, e.g.: gardening, farming, pet care, music lessons, sports club, arts club, board-games club, tourist/hiking club, car club or any other hobby club.

How Much Will You Share About Yourself?

You don't have to be ashamed of your past with JWs. Still, it doesn't mean you have to speak about it and that you have to share it immediately. The principle applies: **When in doubt, leave it out.**

Remember: Once you say something to somebody, that somebody might relay that information to somebody else.

Therefore, if you tell your colleague at work that you are planning to leave JWs and ask him not to tell anybody, eventually, he will tell somebody anyway. People are just unable to keep a secret. Be ready for that.

If you want to keep a secret, don't tell anybody. Keep it to yourself. Once you say something, you cannot take it back. But you can always decide to postpone saying anything. You can just remain quiet and say it later, if you want.

Another reason is: Some people might have heard all kinds of things and they just might not like meeting somebody from a cultish background. This way, you might miss making new friends just by being too open, too soon. Timing is key here.

On other occasions you might feel that you really want to share your past with some people and the challenge that is ahead of you as you are leaving the JWs. You might feel they could be helpful, so you want to be more open with them.

Bear in mind that many new people that you will meet already have an extensive network of friends. They might not understand that you are about to lose *all your present* friends; this is just something completely beyond their thinking. Therefore, it might help you if you don't expect too much from them.

> *Happy are those who never expect anything from anybody since such ones will never be disappointed.*

Some are irreligious and any talk about religion might put them off. Better accept it and enjoy talking with them about topics they like. You might find it very refreshing and you might realize how nice these people are even though they say they don't believe in anything.

Again, don't expect much in any way. Then you can only be pleasantly surprised.

Building Your Support Network

A good approach is to be close friends with a JW couple or a JW that is still viewed as a member but who also intends to get out of the organization. The intent is not to support each other in negativity but to encourage each other to exit with a peace of mind together with your spouse and family members.

Basically, you should be adding new friends to your network each week, step by step. This will make you feel very good since you will see that the people from the "world" are no worse than JWs, in fact, you might be surprised how many new nice people will be coming into your life as you will be opening up to a non-JW world.

You should have a strong, solid support network of friends *long before* you leave JWs for good. This will make the exit for you, your spouse and your family members much easier. Many of these new friends might be happy to help you as an exiting JW with many things. Just be open with them so that they understand what exiting the organization of JWs means. Again, timing is key here.

You can also use our free support and tools from www.FreeFlowPal.com

Don't Stay Lonely

This chapter is extremely important if you are an introverted person. **Introverts** usually do not have many friends and it usually takes them a longer time to make new friends. If you disassociate yourself or if you get disfellowshipped as an introvert—you might end up being very lonely!

✱ Understanding the Main Points

- Where do you already know people that you can get closer to?
- What other possibilities do you have to create new friendships easily?
- How much, if anything, do you want to share about yourself and when do you want to do it?

✱ Taking My Time to Reflect <Ask 10–100 times>

- How easily can I (and our family) make new friends?
- How easy can it be for me to share (or not to share) things about my past with JWs?
- Which approach will create more?

— ••●•• —

Appendix

The Appendix Covers These Topics:

- **No Governing Body or Central Authority in the Bible**
  Five ways to disprove it using the New World Translation (NWT).

- **1914 and the Book of Haggai**
  Why Jerusalem was not destroyed in 607 B.C.E. but in 586/587 B.C.E., using the NWT only.
  This shows that the teaching about the year 1914 is just made up by the Watchtower.

- **Ruse: More Details**
  We will see more details about the ruse used by Gibeonites, Jehu, Joseph, Rebekah, Laban and Leah.

— ••●•• —

71

No Governing Body or Central Authority in the Bible

Briefly: Five ways to disprove it using the New World Translation (NWT).

Governing body, the faithful and discreet slave, central authority, centralized authority, organization.

This is a decisive topic for Jehovah's Witnesses. The WT claims that "Christ chose a small number of men out of the slave class to serve as a visible governing body":

> "While all anointed Christians collectively form God's household, there is abundant evidence that Christ chose a small number of men out of the slave class to serve as a visible governing body… By the year 49 C.E. at the latest, the governing body had been expanded to include not only the remaining apostles but also a number of other older men in Jerusalem. (Acts 15:2) So the makeup of the governing body was not rigidly fixed, but God evidently guided things so that it changed to fit the circumstances of his people. Christ, the active Head of the congregation, used this enlarged governing body to settle the important doctrinal matter of non-Jewish Christians' being circumcised and submitting to the Law of Moses." [w90 3/15 pp. 10-14]

The Watchtower claims that such a governing body operated organizationally as a centralized authority, exercising direction internationally from Jerusalem over all those first-century congregations.

This cannot be substantiated from the Bible, though.

This fact must first be absolutely clear to you. Only then can you start helping your spouse, your family members and your loved ones to see it the same way.

To disprove this unbiblical notion, we will use only:

- New World Translation, and
- Maps (e.g. produced by the Watchtower).

No Governing Body: Five Ways to Disprove It From the NWT

We will deal with this topic from different angles and in five different ways, from the simplest and shortest to extremely thorough:

1/5 No Governing Body: Using the Maps

2/5 No Governing Body: Paul's Missionary Journeys

3/5 No Governing Body: Paul's Four Trips to Jerusalem

4/5 No Governing Body: Selected Parts from Acts 9–28

5/5 No Governing Body: Thorough Study of Acts 9–15

Please, weigh which approach to use with your JW family members to free them from the Watchtower.

—— ••●•• ——

1/5 No Governing Body: Using the Maps

You can suggest to your family that it could be great to have a look together at the Missionary Journeys of apostle Paul.

This is the simplest, shortest and fastest way to show there was nothing like a "governing body" or central authority in the first century C.E.

You will need only the maps of Paul's Missionary Journeys.

You can find them in:

- Book: *Insight on the Scriptures* from the Watchtower
- Website of JWs: www.jw.org or at https://wol.jw.org [go to: New World Translation of the Holy Scriptures 2013 / APPENDIX B / B13 / The Spread of Christianity]
- Viz.bible website: https://viz.bible/journeys/
- Conforming website: http://bit.ly/paulmaps / bit.ly/paulmaps
- Or use links to all these maps at: www.FreeFlowPal.com

What Can You Show?

All three of Paul's major missionary journeys started in Antioch in Syria, not in Jerusalem!

Paul didn't ask anybody to be authorized for any of these journeys. He acted independently. The brothers in Jerusalem learned about Paul's journeys only much later.

- Journey #1 started and ended in Antioch.
- Journey #2 started and ended in Antioch.
- Journey #3 started in Antioch and ended in Jerusalem.

* * *

- Journey #4 Paul was taken from Jerusalem to Rome as a prisoner.
- Journey #5 was from Rome to Spain.

TIP: To show it well, always prefer a map that shows just one journey, not all journeys together. Discuss where the journey started and where it ended.

———— ••●•• ————

2/5 No Governing Body:
Paul's Missionary Journeys

If maps are not enough, you can combine maps and Bible reading.

Again, you can suggest to your family that it could be great to follow the Missionary Journeys of apostle Paul together to really visualize what he was doing, where he was etc.

You can read the full accounts or just verses that show the start and end of each journey.

All three of Paul's major missionary journeys started in Antioch in Syria, not in Jerusalem!

Paul's Missionary Journeys in Acts

1st Journey ::: Acts 13:1–14:28; c. 47-48

Start: *Antioch in Syria*; Ac 13:1–3
End: *Antioch in Syria*; Ac 14:26–28

2nd Journey ::: Acts 15:36–18:22; c. 49–52

Start: *Antioch in Syria*; Ac 15:35-40
End: *Antioch in Syria*; Ac 18:22

3rd Journey ::: Acts 18:22–21:17; c. 52–56

Start: *Antioch in Syria*; Ac 18:22
End: Jerusalem in Palestine; Ac 21:15–17

4th Journey ::: to Rome as a Prisoner; Acts 21:27-28:31

Start: Jerusalem in Palestine; Ac 21:27 (23:11); through Ceasarea, Ac 23:23
End: Rome; Ac 28:16

5th Journey ::: to Spain; Romans 15:22-24, 28

Start: Rome; Rom 15:22
End: Spain; Rom 15:28

——— ••●•• ———

3/5 No Governing Body: Paul's Four Trips to Jerusalem

From what we can see in our Bibles, Paul went to Jerusalem only four times. After his conversion in Damascus (Acts 9), Paul first went to Arabia (Gal 1:17), and then he returned to Damascus.

It took full three years after his conversion, before Paul went to Jerusalem!

Bet even during this visit, he stayed with Cephas (Peter) for 15 days but he did not see any of the other apostles, only James, the brother of the Lord. (Gal 1:17-19)

> Gal 1:17-19; NWT: Nor did I go up to Jerusalem to those who were apostles before I was, but I went to Arabia, and then I returned to Damascus. 18 Then three years later I went up to Jerusalem to visit Cephas, and I stayed with him for 15 days. 19 But I did not see any of the other apostles, only James the brother of the Lord.

Paul apparently worked independently of Jerusalem. He never asked anybody to be authorized for any of his activities.

Paul's base was in Antioch in Syria. He started and ended his 1st and 2nd Missionary Journey in Antioch. Paul also started his 3rd Missionary Journey in Antioch, ended it in Jerusalem.

Paul's first trip to Jerusalem: It took place *three years after* his conversion in Damascus. (Acts 9:25; Acts 9:26 <+**Gal 1:18** cross reference in the NWT>.

Paul's second trip to Jerusalem: Paul and Barnabas brought relief funds to Jerusalem from Antioch in Syria (Acts 11:28-30). The disciples in Antioch acted from their own will, "to what they could afford." No centralized authority was telling them what to do.

Paul's third trip to Jerusalem: It took place *after 14 years*. Paul was not summoned to go to Jerusalem but went there "as a result of a revelation." (Gal 2:1-2)

> Gal 2:1-2; NWT: Then after 14 years I again went up to Jerusalem with Barnabas, also taking Titus along with me. 2 I went up *as a result of a revelation,* and I presented to them the good news that I am preaching among the nations.

Paul's fourth, final trip to Jerusalem: It took place during the latter part of Paul's third missionary journey as recorded in Rom 15:25-28, 1Cor 16:1-4 and Acts 21:15-18. Paul and others carried a gathered contribution for the needy brothers and sisters in the congregation in Jerusalem.

It is clear that apostle Paul acted independently of Jerusalem and that there was no central authority over there or anywhere else.

——··●··——

4/5 No Governing Body:
Selected Parts From Acts 9–28

Please, find below the most important passages from Acts 9–28 that disprove any notion of any centralized authority ("governing body") in the first century.

Acts 9

9:1-2 ::: Saul asks the high priest in Jerusalem *for authorizing letters* to the synagogues in Damascus to arrest the Jewish believers who started calling on the name of Jesus Christ. Saul/Paul knew that for some activities he needed to be authorized. Interestingly, he never asked anybody to be authorized for any of his activities (missionary journeys, letters etc.).

9:10-17 ::: Ananias, a believer from Damascus [not someone from the apostles or elders], lays his hands on Saul.

9:19-25 ::: Saul begins preaching in Damascus [*without first asking anybody to be authorized to do so*]. Compare Ac 9:1-2.

9:26-29 ::: Saul is in Jerusalem, *three years after* his conversion in Damascus; sees only Cephas (Peter) and James (see Gal 1:17-19). There is a break of three years between Act 9:25 and Ac 9:26.

Acts 11

11:26 ::: The disciples were called Christians firstly *in Antioch* [not in Jerusalem!].

Acts 13

13:1-3 ::: **1st Missionary Journey:** Paul and Barnabas are sent as missionaries *from Antioch, not from Jerusalem!* And they *return to Antioch* (14:26–28).

Acts 15

This is the chapter that the Watchtower uses to prove their centralized authority ("governing body"). So, you need to read it very carefully.

15:1 ::: Men from Judea wanted the believers in Antioch to be circumcised according to the Law of Moses.

15:2-3 ::: The congregation in Antioch decided to send Paul, Barnabas and other believers to Jerusalem to talk to apostles and elders.

15:4-5 ::: In Jerusalem, they were *welcomed by the whole congregation, including the apostles and elders.*

15:6-21 ::: Elders and apostles meet together, probably *dozens of men*, not just a small "body" of men. (15:6)

15:22-29 ::: The apostles and the elders [probably *dozens of men*] wrote a letter.

15:22 ::: "The (1) apostles and (2) the elders, together with (3) the whole congregation, decided to send chosen men from among them to Antioch, along with Paul and Barnabas." This could mean that "the whole congregation" (men and women, brothers and sisters) made something like a resolution to show that they agreed with this decision. This is not a model used by the "governing body" of JWs.

15:23 ::: The letter was written to Gentile believers in Antioch, Syria and Cilicia, only. Not to all the cities where Paul started new congregations before.

There are no other similar meetings and decisions described in Acts or in the Christian Greek Scriptures. There are no other similar letters described in Acts or in the Christian Greek Scriptures as being written by the apostles and the elders in Jerusalem. (Thus, we lack "two witnesses".)

On the other hand, we know that Paul wrote his letters to the congregations that he started (up to 14 letters are attributed to Paul).

Paul never asked anybody for his letters to be authorized before he sent them to these congregations.

15:28-29 ::: Only four requirements were in the letter: things to abstain from (idols, blood, strangled, immorality). This is a sole occurrence of such a meeting, decision and letter. Nothing similar occurred again. Compare this to frequent letters from the "governing body" of JWs with many changing requirements.

15:36-41 ::: **2nd Missionary Journey:** Paul starts again *from Antioch* (not from Jerusalem), but without Barnabas. "Paul selected Silas." Paul did not ask anybody who he could take with him. "Barnabas took Mark along and sailed away to Cyprus," without asking anybody to be authorized to do so. At the end of his 2nd missionary journey, Paul *returns to Antioch* (18:22), not to Jerusalem.

Background

Jerusalem was the logical place to go for this particular issue. Not because it would be the location of some kind of international administrative body. It was *primarily because Jerusalem itself was the source of the troublesome problem* that Paul and Barnabas had encountered in Antioch where they were based. Things had been relatively peaceful in Antioch until "men from Jerusalem" came down and caused trouble by their insistence that Gentile Christians should be circumcised and obey the Law. (Acts 15:1, 2, 5, 24).

The troublemakers in Antioch were Jerusalem-based men. These factors, and not solely the presence of the apostles, made Jerusalem the natural site for discussion and settlement of this particular problem. The presence of divinely selected apostles was obviously a factor worth considering. Yet that circumstance was due to end as the apostles died and left no successors—no one with apostolic gifts and authority. So the situation in the middle of the first century involved factors that were not of a permanent or continuing nature and that are simply not applicable in our time.

Moreover, it's a fact that even when the apostles were alive and in Jerusalem, apostle Paul clearly did not view those apostles in Jerusalem as a "governing body" in the sense of an international administrative center, a "headquarters organization." Paul never asked anybody in Jerusalem or anywhere else to authorize any of his activities (compare with Ac 9:1-2).

Acts 9–28: Main Points

From the account in the books of Acts it is quite clear that the congregations acted independently (e.g. Antioch, Jerusalem, Galatia, Corinth etc.) and even the missionaries acted independently without even thinking about authorization from anybody (e.g. Paul, Barnabas, John Mark, Silas, Stephen, Philip etc.).

We do not have any proof when it comes to any notion of a "governing body" or any centralized authority in the book of Acts. However, we have way more than "two or three witnesses" against this teaching:

- Paul did ask for the letters from the high priest to be authorized to arrest those who "called on the name of Jesus" in Damascus (Ac 9:1-2). But Paul never asked to be authorized to carry out any of his activities from anybody and by anybody, not even from Jerusalem.

- Paul never viewed Jerusalem as any place with any authority.

- Paul was sent to his missionary journeys from Antioch, not from Jerusalem.

- It was not in Jerusalem but in Antioch where the disciples were called Christians for the first time. (Acts 11:26)

- Paul did not contact brothers in Jerusalem after his conversion to be authorized as "an apostle to the Gentiles." (Ac 9:15; Rom 11:13). After his conversion, it took *three years* before he went to Jerusalem! (Ac 9:26; Gal 1:17-19)

- Christ said absolutely nothing to Paul (Saul) about going to Jerusalem. Instead of sending him back to Jerusalem, from which city Paul had just come, Christ sent him to bear his name "to the nations as well as to kings" (Acts 9:15).

- Christ gave instructions to Paul through Ananias from Damascus who was clearly not a member of any Jerusalem-based central "governing body." (Acts 9:1-17; 22:5-16).

- Paul was carrying out his initial missionary activities *for three years* (Ac 9:25 vs. 9:26; Gal 1:18) without asking to be authorized from or by anybody, not even anybody from Jerusalem. And he never asked to be authorized by anybody even after these three years.

- The decision in Acts 15 to send chosen men to Antioch was made by (1) the apostles and (2) the elders, (3) together with the whole congregation. (Ac 15:22) Thus, the decision was not made by a small "body" of men, but it was made by dozens, "together with the whole congregation"— which could mean that "the whole congregation" (men and women, brothers and sisters) made something like a resolution to show that they were in agreement with this decision.

- Thus, the meeting and letter in Acts 15 was a one-off occasion that served a very particular issue (circumcision).

- There is no other similar meeting described in the New Testament. There is no other similar letter sent by the apostles and the elders together with the whole congregation.

- On the other hand, apostle Paul wrote and sent many letters to many congregations without asking to be authorized to do so by any centralized authority.

Thus, there was no centralized authority, no "governing body" in the first century: it was not in Jerusalem, it wasn't in Antioch, and it wasn't anywhere else.

—— ••●•• ——

If none of these four shorter approaches could work in your family, you still have option "5/5 No Governing Body: Thorough Study of Acts." See below.

—— ••●•• ——

5/5 No Governing Body:
Thorough Study of Acts 9–15

Reading and Outlining Together

Hopefully, you have already started reading the Bible chronologically together with all your family.

Try to motivate your JW family members to start using these three steps:

1. Let's first read the whole chapter at one go, taking turns by paragraphs.
2. After that, each one of us can try to make his or her own outline. We can read our outlines and make the final, best outline together.
3. In the end, we can go back and read the most important verses and passages together again.

An effective way to dismantle any notion of centralized authority ("governing body") is to read and discuss with your loved ones the account in the books of Acts. Not to arouse any suspicion, you need to read the whole book of Acts together, starting from Acts chapter one.

Ideally, you should have begun *reading the Bible together chronologically* as a family starting from Matthew. In case you didn't, it is a good idea to start with this "outlining" process from Acts 1 (not straight from Acts 9; you would arouse suspicion by this).

Other Approaches

You know your JW family members and you know what could work for them the best. Please, find below some other approaches and try to think about some more of your own:

- Select some passages from Acts 9-15 and bring them up, little by little, step by step.
- "What I am reading here is really interesting." (Without asking about their opinions.)
- "How do you understand this?" (Now, you are asking their opinions, e.g. about Antioch.)
- Highlight or mark these passages in your Bible and let it open somewhere visibly.
- Study the role of Antioch (it was Paul's base, not Jerusalem) and talk about it with your loved ones.

- Say you would like to visit Antakya in modern Turkey because it was the Antioch that used to be Paul's base.
- Your idea: ....

Remember: It's not important to win over your JW family members with your arguments but to win them over.

Outlines of Acts With Sample Questions for Discussion

Please, find below a procedure that you can use when reading from the book of Acts together with your spouse and your family members. Hopefully, they will be able to see by themselves that God never used any centralized authority ("governing body").

What you will need:

- The Bible with cross-references (e.g. *NWT: The New World Translation*)
- A map with Paul's missionary trips, in the Bible or online (so you can visualize the places and distances between them). Stress to your JW family members the limited ways people in those days could use for traveling. They also had no internet, no printing press, no phones etc. All these facts can help you understand the events better.

Acts 9-15: Antioch or Jerusalem?

You can begin dismantling the authority of the "governing body" starting from Acts 9. That's why any helpful outlines and questions for discussions are here starting only from Acts 9.

Remember: First, the account has to be absolutely clear to you. Well-prepared questions can help you lead the discussion the way you need.

Acts 9

Outline

9:1-2 ::: Saul asks the high priest in Jerusalem to *authorize letters* for the synagogues in Damascus to arrest the Jewish believers who started calling on the name of Jesus Christ. Saul/Paul knew that for some activities he needed to be authorized. Interestingly, he never asked anybody to be authorized for any of his activities (missionary journeys, letters etc.).

9:3-7 ::: Saul is blinded by Jesus Christ near Damascus.

9:10-17 ::: Ananias, a believer from Damascus [not someone from the apostles or elders], lays his hands on Saul.

9:19-25 ::: Saul begins preaching in Damascus [*without first asking anybody to be authorized to do so*]. Compare Ac 9:1-2.

9:26-29 ::: Saul is in Jerusalem, *three years after* his conversion in Damascus; sees only Cephas (Peter) and James (see Gal 1:17-19).

9:31 ::: Congregations in Judea, Galilee and Samaria enjoy peace.

9:32-42 ::: Peter heals Aeneas and raises Dorcas.

Acts 9: Questions for Discussion

Q: Who and why does Saul/Paul ask for letters to the synagogues in Damascus? (Ac 9:1-2)

Acts 9:1-2; NWT: Saul, still breathing threat and murder against the disciples of the Lord, *went to the high priest 2 and asked him for letters to the synagogues in Damascus,* so that he might bring bound to Jerusalem any whom he found who belonged to The Way, both men and women.

Ac 9:13-14; NWT: Ananias answered: "Lord, I have heard from many about this man, about all the harm he did to your holy ones in Jerusalem. 14 And here *he has authority from the chief priests to arrest* all those calling on your name."

Saul/Paul was an educated Pharisee and he *knew that he had to be authorized* to perform some activities. Here, he "asked the high priest for letters to the synagogues in Damascus, so that he might bring bound to Jerusalem" those who "called on" the name of Jesus Christ (Acts 9:21). These were apparently Jewish worshipers who started calling on the name of Jesus which was contrary to the Mosaic Law, contrary to one of the Ten Commandments (Ex 20:3 "You must not have any other gods besides me.").

Remember: Saul/Paul knew that if there was a higher authority from which he would need a permission/letter he would ask such an authority for such permission (as he did in Ac 9:1-2). Interestingly, Paul never asked anybody (not even anybody in Jerusalem) whether, how and where he could carry out his missionary activities. Why not? Apparently, there was no such authority in Jerusalem or anywhere else to be asked.

Q: Where is Paul converted?

A: Paul is converted on his way to Damascus. (Acts 9:2n)

Q: Who lays hands on Saul/Paul?

A: Ananias, a man from Damascus [not any apostle of elder from Jerusalem], lays his hands on Saul/Paul. (Acts 9:17)

Q: Did Paul consider Jerusalem to be the divinely appointed administrative center for his missionary activities?

A: Paul definitely did not consider Jerusalem to be the divinely appointed administrative center for his missionary activities.

Q: Did Paul contact brothers in Jerusalem after his conversion to be "an apostle to the Gentiles?" (Acts 9:15; Romans 11:13).

A: No, Paul did not contact brothers in Jerusalem after his conversion to be "an apostle to the Gentiles." (Acts 9:15; Romans 11:13).

Compare: With notes to Acts 9:2, 13-14 where Saul/Paul asks the high priest for "letters."

Ac 9:15; NWT: But the Lord said to him [to Ananias in Damascus]: "Go! because this man is a chosen vessel to me to bear my name to the nations as well as to kings and the sons of Israel.

Rom 11:13 Now I speak to you who are people of the nations. Seeing that I (Paul) am an apostle to the nations, I glorify my ministry.

Q: Where did Jesus Christ send Saul/Paul after his conversion?

A: Christ said absolutely nothing to Paul (Saul) about going to Jerusalem. Instead of sending him back to Jerusalem, from which city Paul had just come, Christ sent him to bear his name "to the nations as well as to kings" (Acts 9:15).

Q: Through whom did Christ give instructions to Paul?

A: Christ gave instructions to Paul through Ananias from Damascus who was clearly not a member of any Jerusalem-based centralized authority, or "governing body." (Acts 9:1-17; 22:5-16).

Q: How long after his conversion did Paul make his first trip to Jerusalem?

A: There's a paragraph break between verses Acts 9:25 and Acts 9:26 in NWT and most other translations. How much time elapsed between events in Acts 9:25 and events in Acts 9:26?

Ac 9:26-28; NWT: On arriving in Jerusalem, <+**Gal 1:18** cross reference in the NWT> he made efforts to join the disciples, but they were all afraid of him, because they did not believe he was a disciple. 27 So Barnabas came to his aid and led him to the apostles <only Peter and James; see Gal 1:18-19>, and he told them in detail how on the road he had seen the Lord, and that he had spoken to him, and how in Damascus he had spoken boldly in the name of Jesus. 28 So he remained with them, moving about freely in Jerusalem, speaking boldly in the name of the Lord.

NOTE: By saying, "on arriving in Jerusalem," NWT makes it sound in Ac 9:26 as if no time elapsed between events in Acts 9:25 and events in Acts 9:26. Compare NWT translation of Ac 9:26 with WEB translation:

Ac 9:26; WEB: When Saul *had come to Jerusalem,* he tried to join himself to the disciples; but they were all afraid of him, not believing that he was a disciple.

+Gal 1:17-19; NWT: Nor did I [Paul] go up to Jerusalem to those who were apostles before I was, but I went to Arabia, and then I returned to Damascus. 18 Then *three years later* I went up to Jerusalem to visit Cephas, and I stayed with him for 15 days. 19 But *I did not see any of the other apostles,* only James the brother of the Lord.

From Gal 1:17-19 we see that it was not until *three years later* that Paul made a trip to Jerusalem! And he states specifically that at that time he saw only Peter and James the brother of the Lord, but no other apostles during his fifteen-day stay. He was therefore at no "headquarters meeting" directed by a "governing body."

TIP: You can suggest: Since Acts 9:26 has a cross reference to Gal 1:18 in NWT it is a good idea to read the whole letter to Galatians between the verses in Acts 9:25 and 9:26. Galatians 2:1, 2 is very helpful, too, see the discussion about Acts 13 below. Paul wrote his letter to Galatians during his 1st Missionary Journey.

Remember: Paul was carrying out his missionary activities for all these three years without asking to be authorized from or by anybody, not even anybody from Jerusalem.

Acts 10

Outline

10:1-8 ::: Cornelius' vision.

10:9-16 ::: Peter's vision of cleansed animals.

10:17-33 ::: Peter visits Cornelius.

10:34-33 ::: Peter proclaims good news to Gentiles.

10:34-35 ::: "God is not partial."

10:44-48 ::: Gentiles receive holy spirit and get baptized.

Acts 10: Questions for Discussion

Acts 10 do not bring in anything on the topic of "governing body." So, you can just read it, discuss it and make an outline together with your JW family members.

Acts 11

Outline

11:1-18 ::: Peter explains his actions with Gentiles to the apostles, brothers and to the supporters of circumcision.

11:19-30 :::: The congregation in Antioch in Syria (Antakya in modern Turkey).

11:19-21::: The ministry of the Greek-speaking believers.

11:22-26 ::: The ministry of Barnabas.

11:26 ::: The disciples were called Christians firstly in Antioch [not in Jerusalem!].

11:27-30 ::: The disciples determined, each according to what he could afford, to send relief to the brothers living in Judea, sending it to the elders by the hand of Barnabas and Saul.

Acts 11: Questions for Discussion

Q: Doesn't the fact that Peter had to explain that he "went into the house of men who were not circumcised and ate with them" mean that there was some centralized authority?

A: No, it doesn't. It says:

Ac 11:1-4; NWT: Now the apostles and the brothers who were in Judea heard that people of the nations had also accepted the word of God. 2 So when Peter came up to Jerusalem, the supporters of circumcision began to criticize him, 3 saying: "You went into the house of men who were not circumcised and ate with them." 4 At this Peter went on to explain the matter in detail to them.

From the context it is clear that Peter explained this matter primarily to "the supporters of circumcision," while the apostles and brothers were probably present.

Q: Doesn't Acts 11:22 point to some centralized authority in Jerusalem? [There's no need to discuss this, unless questions are raised.]

A: No, it doesn't. It says:

Ac 11: 22; NWT: The report about them (a) reached the ears of the (b) congregation in Jerusalem, and (c) they sent out Barnabas as far as Antioch.

(a) The report ("tidings" in KJV; "account" in YLT) *reached* the ears of the congregation in Jerusalem." It was not requested by anybody from Jerusalem, it was definitely not reported to any centralized authority.

(b) This account reached the ears of the "congregation in Jerusalem," not any centralized authority.

(c) This congregation (not any centralized authority) then sent out Barnabas to Antioch.

NOTE: The word "report" as featured in NWT doesn't mean something requested by a higher authority. The Greek word "logos" [Strong's number G3056] is used in the original text. G3056, "logos" is translated in the following manner in KJV: word (218x), saying (50x), account (8x), speech (8x), Word (Christ) (7x), thing (5x), not translated (2x), miscellaneous (32x).

Q: Where did the Christians get their name?

A: Ac 11:26; NWT: It was first in Antioch that the disciples were by divine providence called Christians.

It was in Antioch, not in Jerusalem!

Q: Doesn't Acts 11:29-30 point to some centralized authority in Jerusalem? [There's no need to discuss this, unless questions are raised.]

A: No, it doesn't. It says:

Ac 11:29-30; NWT: So the disciples determined, each according to what he could afford, to send relief to the brothers living in Judea; 30 and this they did, sending it to the elders by the hand of Barnabas and Saul.

(a) The disciples acted on their own behalf, "to what he could afford." No centralized authority was telling them what to do.

(b) They sent this relief "to the elders" of the congregation in Jerusalem, not to any centralized authority.

Acts 12

Outline

12:1-5 ::: James killed; Peter imprisoned.

12:6-19 ::: Peter miraculously set free.

12:20-25 ::: Herod struck by an angel.

Acts 12: Questions for Discussion

Acts 12 do not bring in anything on the topic of "governing body." So, you can just read it, discuss it and make an outline together with your JW family members.

Acts 13

Outline

13:1-3 ::: **1st Missionary Journey:** Paul and Barnabas are sent as missionaries *from Antioch, not from Jerusalem!* And they *return to Antioch* (14:26–28).

13:4-12 ::: Ministry on Cyprus.

13:13-41 ::: Paul's speech in Antioch of Pisidia.

13:42-52 ::: Prophetic command to turn to the nations.

Acts 13: Questions for Discussion

Q: Where did Paul make his base? From which congregation was he sent?

A: Ac 13:1-3; NWT: Now in Antioch there were prophets and teachers in the local congregation ... 2 The holy spirit said: "Set aside for me Barnabas and Saul for the work to which I have called them." 3 Then after fasting and praying, they laid their hands on them and sent them off.

Paul made his base in Antioch, not in Jerusalem. He engaged in missionary journeys and it was the congregation of Antioch where he was sent from, not Jerusalem. It was a very long period of time before Paul saw any reason or occasion to go to Jerusalem. Paul clarifies this in Galatians 2:1, 2:

Gal 2:1-2; NWT: Then *after 14 years I again went up to Jerusalem* with Barnabas, also taking Titus along with me. 2 *I went up as a result of a revelation.*

Paul states that he went to Jerusalem again "after 14 years" and only "as a result of a revelation." This shows that:

(a) Paul did not view Jerusalem as any seat of centralized authority. He "went up to Jerusalem"—probably to visit the congregation there, the brothers, even some apostles, but definitely not any centralized authority.

(b) Christians did not customarily and routinely look to Jerusalem as a seat of centralized authority for Christian congregations.

(c) Paul was not summoned by anybody from Jerusalem. It took a divine revelation to cause Paul to make this particular trip there.

Acts 14

Outline

14:1-7 ::: Paul and Barnabas meet opposition in Iconium.

14:8-18 ::: Mistaken for gods in Lystra.

14:19-20 ::: Paul survives stoning.

14:21-23 ::: Strengthening the congregations.

14:24-28 ::: **End of the 1st Missionary Journey:** Paul and Barnabas *return to Antioch of Syria, not to Jerusalem*!

Acts 14: Questions for Discussion

Q: Where did Paul and Barnabas return once they completed their 1st Missionary Journey? (Ac 14:24-28)

> A: They went back to Antioch, not to Jerusalem.

> Ac 14: 25-16; NWT: And after proclaiming the word in Perga, they went down to Attalia. 26 From there they sailed off for Antioch, where they had been entrusted to the undeserved kindness of God for the work they had now completed. 27 When they had arrived and had gathered the congregation together, they related the many things God had done by means of them, and that he had opened to the nations the door to faith.

Q: To whom did Paul and Barnabas relate the "many things God had done by means of them, and that he had opened to the nations the door to faith"?

> A: Paul and Barnabas related all this to the congregation in Antioch, not to the apostles or to the elders in Jerusalem.

Acts 15

This is the chapter that the Watchtower uses to prove their centralized authority ("governing body"). So, you need to be really well prepared.

Outline

15:1 ::: Men from Judea wanted the believers in Antioch to be circumcised according to the Law of Moses.

15:2-3 ::: The congregation in Antioch decided to send Paul, Barnabas and other believers to Jerusalem to talk to apostles and elders.

15:4-5 ::: In Jerusalem, they were welcomed by the (1) whole congregation, including (2) the apostles and (3) elders.

15:6-21 ::: Elders and apostles meet together, probably dozens of men, not just a small "body" of men. (15:6)

15:22 ::: "The (1) apostles and (2) the elders, together with (3) the whole congregation, decided to send chosen men from among them to Antioch, along with Paul and Barnabas." This could mean that "the whole congregation" (men and women, brothers and sisters) made something like a resolution to show that they agreed with this decision.

15:22-29 ::: The apostles and the elders [probably dozens of men] wrote a letter.

15:23 ::: The letter was written to Gentile believers in Antioch, Syria and Cilicia, only. Not to all the cities where Paul started new congregations before.

15:28-29 ::: Only four requirements were in the letter: things to abstain from (idols, blood, strangled, immorality). This is a sole occurrence of such a meeting, decision and letter.

15:30-34 ::: Congregations encouraged by the letter.

15:34 ::: Paul and Barnabas stayed in Antioch.

15:36-41 :::: **2nd Missionary Journey:** Paul starts again *from Antioch* (not from Jerusalem), but without Barnabas. "Paul selected Silas." Paul did not ask anybody who he could take with him. "Barnabas took Mark along and sailed away to Cyprus," without asking anybody to be authorized to do so. At the end of his 2nd missionary journey, Paul *returns to Antioch* (18:22), not to Jerusalem.

Background

The account of Acts chapter fifteen shows why Jerusalem was the logical place to go to for this particular issue. Nowhere does the account indicate that Jerusalem was the location of some kind of international administrative body. Rather, *it was primarily because Jerusalem itself was the source of the troublesome problem* that Paul and Barnabas had encountered in Antioch where they were serving. Things had been relatively peaceful in Antioch until "men from Jerusalem" came down and caused trouble by their insistence that Gentile Christians should be circumcised and obey the Law. (Acts 15:1, 2, 5, 24).

The Christian congregation had its beginning in Jerusalem. Judea, with its capital of Jerusalem, was where strong adherence to law-keeping prevailed most intensely among persons professing Christianity, that attitude continuing even for years after this particular meeting was held. (Compare Galatians 2:11-14; Acts 21:15, 18-21). The troublemakers in Antioch were Jerusalem-based men. These factors, and not solely the presence of the apostles, made Jerusalem the natural site for discussion and settlement of this particular problem. The presence of divinely selected apostles was obviously a factor worth considering. Yet that circumstance was due to end as the apostles died and left no successors—no one with apostolic gifts and authority. So the situation in the middle of the first century involved factors that were not of a permanent or continuing nature and that are simply not applicable in our time.

Moreover, the fact remains that, even when the apostles were alive and in Jerusalem, the apostle Paul clearly did not view that apostolic body in Jerusalem as a "governing body" in the sense of an international administrative center, a "headquarters organization."

Acts 15: Questions for Discussion

Q: Who wanted the believers in Antioch to be circumcised according to the Law of Moses?

A: Men from Judea wanted the believers in Antioch to be circumcised according to the Law of Moses. (Ac 15:1)

Q: Why was the meeting not held in Antioch but in Jerusalem?

A: The meeting was held in Jerusalem, because men from Judea (from Jerusalem) wanted the believers in Antioch to be circumcised. Men from Judea (from Jerusalem) were the source of the problem. Thus, the problem was discussed at the place where the problem originated. (Ac 15:2-3)

Q: Who welcomed Paul, Barnabas and others coming from Antioch?

A: In Jerusalem, they were welcomed (1) *by the whole congregation*, including (2) *the apostles* and (3) *elders*. [Not just by a small "body of men."] (Ac 15:4-5)

Q: Who met to discuss the issue?

A: Elders and apostles meet together, probably dozens of men, not just a small "body" of men. (Ac 15:6)

Q: Who were the speakers at this meeting?

A: Only four names are mentioned: Apostle Peter (Ac 15:7); Barnabas and Paul (Ac 15:2) who were sent to Jerusalem by their congregation from Antioch; James, the brother of Jesus (Ac 15:13). Only Peter and James (as speakers) could have been from Jerusalem.

Q: Who decided to send chosen men from among them to Antioch?

A: This decision was made by (1) the apostles and (2) the elders, (3) together with the whole congregation. (Ac 15:22) Thus, the decision was not made by a small "body" of men, but it was made by dozens, "together with the whole congregation"—which could mean that "the whole congregation" (men and women, brothers and sisters) made something like a resolution to show that they agreed with this decision.

Q: Who wrote the letter?

A: The letter was not written by just a small "body" of men; it was written by (1) the apostles and (2) the elders, probably by dozens of men together. (Acts 15:23)

Q: What was written in the letter?

A: Just *four requirements* were stressed, i.e. about things to abstain from: idols, blood, strangled, immorality. (Acts 15:28-29)

NOTE: Compare this to the *frequent letters* written and sent by the "governing body" of JWs to all the congregations of JWs where there are *many requirements*.

Q: To whom was the letter written and sent?

A: The letter was written to Gentile believers in Antioch, Syria and Cilicia, only. (Acts 15:23) Not to all the cities where Paul or Peter started new congregations before. The letter was not sent to: Lydda, Ac 9:32; Phoenicia, Cyprus, Ac 11:19; Caesarea, Acts 10:24; to Damascus, Salamis, Paphos, Perga, Pamphylia, Iconium, Lystra, Derbe and other cities from Paul's 1st Missionary Journey. This shows that the letter was sent only to the areas where the "men from Judea" had been stressing the issue of circumcision before.

Q: How many witnesses do we need from the Scriptures to establish some teaching?

A: The Watchtower itself stresses the rule of "two witnesses":

2Co 13:1; NWT: "On the testimony of two or three witnesses every matter must be established." (Also: De 17:6; 19:15; Mt 18:6; 1Tim 5:19; Re 11:3)

Q: How many similar meetings are described in Acts or in the Christian Greek Scriptures?

A: None. There are no other similar meetings described in Acts or in the Christian Greek Scriptures. (Thus, we lack "two witnesses".)

Q: How many similar (important) decisions are described in Acts or in the Christian Greek Scriptures as being decided by the apostles and the elders in Jerusalem?

A: None. There are no other similar decisions described in Acts or in the Christian Greek Scriptures. (Thus, we lack "two witnesses".)

Q: How many similar (important) letters are described in Acts or in the Christian Greek Scriptures as being written by the apostles and the elders in Jerusalem?

A: None. There are no other similar letters described in Acts or in the Christian Greek Scriptures as being written by the apostles and the elders in Jerusalem. (Thus, we lack "two witnesses".)

On the other hand, we know that Paul wrote his letters to the congregations that he started.

Q: Who did Paul ask for his letters to be authorized before he sent them to the congregations he visited during his missionary journeys?

A: Paul never asked anybody for his letters to be authorized before he sent them to these congregations.

Q: Where did Paul and Barnabas stay after delivering the letter referenced in Acts 15:23?

A: Paul and Barnabas stayed in Antioch. After delivering the letter, they did not return to Jerusalem. It shows that they did not view Jerusalem as any central place with some authority.

Q: From where does Paul start his 2nd Missionary Journey?

A: Paul starts his 2nd Missionary Journey as his 1st Missionary Journey— from Antioch. (Acts 15:35-41) Paul does not start from Jerusalem. This again shows that he did not view Jerusalem as any central place with some authority. "Paul selected Silas." Paul did not ask anybody who he could take with him. "Barnabas took Mark along and sailed away to Cyprus," without asking anybody to be authorized to do so. At the end of his 2nd missionary journey, Paul *returns to Antioch* (18:22), not to Jerusalem.

Acts: Questions and Observations

Just to be on the safe side, more observations are below, in case your JW family members ask more questions or have some doubts. Please, read on to be ready for their questions.

Authority of Jerusalem?

Q: Didn't Jerusalem have a central authority, anyway?

A: We need to bear in mind that the Christian congregation had its beginning in Jerusalem.

There was a congregation with the elders.

Still, even when the apostles were alive and in Jerusalem (probably a only a relatively short time together, because of persecution), apostle Paul clearly did not view these apostles as any centralized authority

From Gal 1:17-19 we see that only *three years* after his conversion Paul made a trip to Jerusalem! And he states specifically that at that time he saw only Peter and James the brother of the Lord, but *no other apostles during his fifteen-day stay*. He was therefore at no "headquarters meeting" directed by a "governing body."

There was apparently no central authority. It is clear that Paul and Barnabas acted independently:

> Acts 15:39-41; NWT: There was a sharp burst of anger, so that they (Paul and Barnabas) separated from each other; and Barnabas took Mark along and sailed away to Cyprus. 40 Paul selected Silas and departed after he had been entrusted by the brothers to the undeserved kindness of Jehovah. 41 He went through Syria and Cilicia, strengthening the congregations.

Barnabas didn't ask anybody to be authorized to go to Cyprus and to take Mark along with him.

Paul didn't ask anybody to be authorized to go to Syria and Cilicia and to take Silas along with him.

Apostles Together

Q: How about the passages where we read that the "apostles were together"?

A: The short answer is: This just means that they were together. They stayed together while walking with Jesus and also after his resurrection. There's no reason to read into it any further.

The apostles had gone into Galilee after Christ's resurrection. But before he ascended he told them to stay in Jerusalem until Pentecost, which came about 10 days after his ascension. After Pentecost it appears that they stayed in Jerusalem.

> Acts 1:3; NWT: After he had suffered, he showed himself alive to them by many convincing proofs. He was seen by them throughout 40 days, and he was speaking about the Kingdom of God. 4 While he was meeting with them, he ordered them: "Do not leave Jerusalem, but keep waiting for what the Father has promised, about which you heard from me."

Eventually, persecution scattered the newly converted Christians throughout Judea, Samaria, and the Jewish diaspora.

> Acts 8:1; NWT: Saul, for his part, approved of his murder. On that day great persecution arose against the congregation that was in Jerusalem; *all except the apostles were scattered* throughout the regions of Judea and Samaria.

The apostles stayed in Jerusalem but we don't know for how long. We shouldn't imagine that under the conditions of persecution they could be together for a long time. What's more, in those days, they didn't have any electronic means of communication that we have today. They depended on personal communication and hand-written letters which could take weeks or months to be delivered from place to place. Also, they wanted to teach people in other regions about Jesus Christ. In time, various apostles went to visit these scattered groups. It is known that most apostles suffered a violent death.

We can get some information from Hippolytus (c. 170–235 AD), one of the most important second-third century Christian writers. Hippolytus writes in his work *On the Twelve Apostles of Christ*:

Where each of them preached, and where he met his end.

1. Peter preached the Gospel in Pontus, and Galatia, and Cappadocia, and Betania, and Italy, and Asia, after which he was crucified by Nero in Rome with his head downward, as he himself desired to suffer in that manner.

2. Andrew preached to the Scythians and Thracians, and was crucified, suspended on an olive tree, at Patra, [a town] of Achaia; and there too he was buried.

3. John, again, in Asia, was banished by Domitian the king to the isle of Patmos, in which also he wrote his Gospel and saw the apocalyptic vision; and in Trajan's time he fell asleep at Ephesus, where his remains were sought for, but could not be found.

4. James, his brother, when preaching in Judea, was cut down by the sword by Herod the tetrarch, and was buried there.

5. Philip preached in Phrygia, and was crucified in Hierapolis with his head downward in the time Domitian, and was buried there.

6. Bartholomew, again, [preached] to the Indians, to whom he also gave the Gospel according to Matthew, [and] was crucified with his head downward, and was buried in Allanum, [a town] of Parthia.

7. And Matthew wrote the Gospel in the Hebrew tongue, and published it in Jerusalem, and fell asleep in Hierees, [a town] of Parthia.

8. And Thomas preached to the Parthians, Medes, Persians, Hyrcanians, Bactrians, and Margians, and was thrust through in the four members of his body with a pine spear at Calamene, the city of India, and was buried there.

9. And James the son of Alphaus, when preaching in Jerusalem, was stoned to death by the Jews, and was buried there beside the temple.

10. Jude, who is also [called] Lebbaus, preached to the people of Edessa, and to all Mesopotamia, and fell asleep at Berytus, and was buried there.

11. Simon the Zealot, the son of Clopas, who is also [called] Jude, became bishop of Jerusalem after James the Just, and fell asleep and was buried there at the age of 120.

12. And Matthias, who was one of the seventy, was numbered along with the eleven apostles, and preached in Jerusalem, and fell asleep and was buried there.

13. And Paul entered into the apostleship a year after the assumption of Christ; and beginning in Jerusalem, he advanced as far as Illyricum, and Italy, and Spain, preaching the Gospel for five-and-thirty years. And in the time of Nero he was beheaded in Rome, and was buried there.

Teaching of the Apostles

Q: But the teaching was carried out by the apostles. Doesn't this show some centralized authority?

A: Who else could initially teach others about Jesus than the apostles who were walking with him during his earthly ministry? But what did the apostles teach about? They were teaching the people the simple Gospel about Jesus Christ and about his resurrection.

Ac 2:42; NWT: And they continued devoting themselves to the *teaching of the apostles,* to associating together, to the taking of meals, and to prayers.

Ac 2:43; NWT: Many wonders and signs began to occur through the apostles [to witness about Jesus Christ, see Ac 2:38].

Ac 4:2; NWT: The apostles were *teaching* the people and were openly *declaring the resurrection of Jesus from the dead.*

Ac 4:33; NWT: And with great power *the apostles continued giving the witness about the resurrection of the Lord Jesus.*

Apostles Laid Their Hands on Disciples

Q: But the apostles laid their hands on disciples, for example in Acts 6:6; 8:17. Doesn't this show some centralized authority?

Ac 6:6; NWT: They brought them to the apostles, and after praying, they laid their hands on them.

Ac 8:17; NWT: Then they (the apostles) laid their hands on them, and they began to receive holy spirit.

A: No, this doesn't show any centralized authority. Many others laid their hands on disciples; this act never showed any centralized authority.

Ananias laid his hands on Saul:

Ac 9:17; NWT: So Ananias went and entered the house, and he laid his hands on him and said: "Saul, brother, the Lord Jesus, who appeared to you on the road along which you were coming, has sent me so that you may recover sight and be filled with holy spirit."

The brothers in Antioch laid their hands on Paul and Barnabas:

Ac 13:3; NWT: Then after fasting and praying, they <the brothers in Antioch> laid their hands on them <on Paul and Barnabas> and sent them off.

Paul laid his hands on disciples in Ephesus:

Ac 19:6; NWT: And when Paul laid his hands on them, the holy spirit came upon them, and they began speaking in foreign languages and prophesying.

Paul laid his hands on the father of Publius:

Ac 28:8; NWT: It so happened that the father of Publius was lying in bed sick with fever and dysentery, and Paul went in to him and prayed, laid his hands on him, and healed him.

Apostles Sent Others to Preach

Q: The apostles were sending others to preach to some areas. Doesn't this show some centralized authority? An example of that is in Acts 8:14; NWT: "When the apostles in Jerusalem heard that Samaria had accepted the word of God, they sent Peter and John to them."

A: The most obvious meaning is: The apostles heard about it, and from their midst they chose and sent the apostles Peter and John. This doesn't show any centralized authority.

In a similar way, Paul and Barnabas were sent by the congregation in Antioch. (Ac 13:1-3) Paul was sent to his missionary journeys from Antioch, not from Jerusalem.

Acts: Summary

We have to rely on the book of Acts, from which we do not see any centralized authority. From the account in the books of Acts it is quite clear that the congregations acted independently (e.g. Antioch, Jerusalem, Galatia, Corinth etc.) and even the missionaries acted independently without even thinking about authorization from anybody (e.g. Paul, Barnabas, John Mark, Silas, Stephen, Philip etc.).

We do not have one single witness when it comes to any notion of "governing body" or any centralized authority in the book of Acts. But we have way more than "two or three witnesses" against this teaching:

- Paul did ask for the letters from the high priest to be authorized to arrest those who "called on the name of Jesus" in Damascus (Ac 9:1-2). But Paul never asked to be authorized to carry out any of his activities from anybody and by anybody, not even from Jerusalem.

- Paul never viewed Jerusalem as any place with any authority.

- Paul was sent to his Missionary Journeys from Antioch, not from Jerusalem.

- It was not in Jerusalem but in Antioch where the disciples were called Christians for the first time. (Acts 11:26)

- Paul did not contact brothers in Jerusalem after his conversion to be authorized as "an apostle to the Gentiles." (Acts 9:15; Romans 11:13). After his conversion, he first went to Jerusalem after three years!

- Christ said absolutely nothing to Paul (Saul) about going to Jerusalem. Instead of sending him back to Jerusalem, the city from which Paul had just come, Christ sent him to bear his name "to the nations as well as to kings" (Acts 9:15).

- Christ gave instructions to Paul through Ananias from Damascus who was clearly not a member of any Jerusalem-based central "governing body." (Acts 9:1-17; 22:5-16).

- Paul was carrying out his initial missionary activities *for three years* (Ac 9:25 vs. 9:26; Gal 1:18) without asking to be authorized from or by anybody, not even anybody from Jerusalem. And he never asked to be authorized any time after these three years.

- The decision in Acts 15 to send chosen men to Antioch was made by (1) the apostles and (2) the elders, (3) together with the whole congregation. (Ac 15:22) Thus, the decision was not made by a small "body" of men, but it was made by dozens, "together with the whole congregation"— which could mean that "the whole congregation" (men and women, brothers and sisters) made something like a resolution to show that they were in agreement with this decision.

- Thus, the meeting and letter in Acts 15 was a one-off occasion that served a very particular issue (circumcision).

- There is no other similar meeting described in the New Testament. There is no other similar letter sent by the apostles and the elders together with the whole congregation.

- On the other hand, apostle Paul wrote and sent many letters to many congregations without asking to be authorized to do so by any centralized authority.

100

Thus, there was no centralized authority (no "governing body") in the first century: it was not in Jerusalem, not in Antioch, and not anywhere else.

The Watchtower claims to have their "governing body" according to the model from the first century. But this claim cannot be substantiated from the Scriptures.

We don't find *the term* "governing body" (or any term suggesting centralized authority) in the New Testament, we don't find *any model* of any centralized authority in the Scriptures, either.

If there is any centralized authority (or "governing body") at this time, it is a self-appointed and self-serving institution. Thus, there's no need to listen to it, obey it, follow it, serve it or to be afraid of it.

Note

Hopefully, the ideas presented were sufficient. It might be a good idea to use just those that will be understandable by your JW members.

Remember: It's not important to win over your JW family members with your arguments but to win them over.

— ··●·· —

How Haggai Disproves 1914

This Topic Has Two Parts

- **How Haggai Disproves 1914: The Main Facts** about the wrong dating of the destruction of Jerusalem to 607 B.C.E., therefore the wrong dating of 1914 C.E.

- **How Haggai Disproves 1914: Auxiliary Information** where you can see how the Watchtower calculates 2520 years from 607 B.C.E. to arrive at 1914 C.E.

One of the main teachings of the Watchtower is that "Jesus Christ began to rule as King of God's Kingdom in 1914." The year of 1914 is full of meaning for JWs.

It supposedly means that Jesus's "presence" on Earth began in 1914, therefore JWs must be active to preach about this event and about the imminent end of "this system of things", about the coming God's war at Armageddon and about the new world in God's Paradise.

To arrive at 1914, the Watchtower starts from the destruction of Jerusalem which JWs date to 607 B.C.E., whereas all the authorities date this event to 586/587 B.C.E.

Why 607 B.C.E. and 1914 C.E. Is Wrong

We will see that 607 B.C.E. is wrong, therefore 1914 is wrong, too,

The Watchtower states that Jerusalem was destroyed in 607 B.C.E.

> "The city walls (of Jerusalem) were breached on Tammuz 9, 607 B.C.E. A month later, on Ab 10, Nebuchadnezzar's agent, Nebuzaradan, entered the conquered city and began demolition work, burning the temple and other buildings and proceeding to pull down the city walls. Jerusalem's king and most of her people were exiled to Babylon and her treasures were carried away as plunder." [it-2 pp. 39-49, *Jerusalem*]

Moreover, the Watchtower calculates 2520 years from 607 B.C.E. to arrive at 1914 C.E. as the year that was supposedly prophetically marked:

"God's representative rulership on earth was to cease its operation, as happened in 607 B.C.E.—but not indefinitely... At the end of that period, Jehovah would give rulership to the legal heir, Jesus Christ... Counting 2,520 years from 607 B.C.E. brings us to 1914 C.E. That is the year when "the appointed times of the nations," or seven times, ended. This means that Jesus Christ began to rule as King of God's Kingdom in 1914. [w06 7/15 pp. 4-7, *God's Kingdom—Superior in Every Way*]

— ••●•• —

How Haggai Disproves 1914: The Main Facts

Notice what we learn from the very beginning of the book of Haggai:

> Haggai 1:1-2; NWT: In *the second year of King Darius,* in the sixth month, on the first day of the month, the word of Jehovah came through Haggai the prophet to Zerubbabel son of Shealtiel, the governor of Judah, and to Joshua son of Jehozadak, the high priest, saying: 2 "This is what Jehovah of armies says, 'These people say, "The time has not yet come for the house of Jehovah to be built."'"

King Darius (Darius I) ruled 521-486 B.C.E. Haggai wrote his book "in the second year of King Darius," which was in 520 B.C.E. The Watchtower uses the same dating for the book of Haggai as all the other sources.

Who Could Have Remembered the "Former Temple"?

There were "some of the Jews who returned from the exile and who had seen the former temple of Solomon." We know this from Haggai 2:3.

> **Haggai 2:3; NWT:** *Who is left among you who saw this house in its former glory?* How does it look to you now? Does it not seem like nothing in comparison?

These could not have been just few individuals since Ezra (a contemporary of Haggai) brings out that "many ... had seen the former house":

> **Ezra 3:12; NWT:** *Many of the priests, the Levites,* and the heads of the paternal houses—the old men *who had seen the former house*—wept with a loud voice when they saw the foundation of this house being laid, while many others shouted joyfully at the top of their voice.

From all the Israelites, only about 200,000 men, women and children took the long journey from Babylon back to Jerusalem. It would take about four months to traverse nearly 900 miles (1,450 km). Some were simply too old to undertake this long and strenuous journey.

Let's have a little recap.

We are in 520 B.C.E. Haggai is addressing those who remembered the former temple. Ezra even brings out that "many of the priests, the Levites, and the heads of the paternal houses—the old men ... had seen the former house." If any of these were *born* in 607 B.C.E., they would have been 87 years old in 520 B.C.E., but then they could not have remembered the former temple.

607 B.C.E. (97 years old)

How old would these Jews have to be to remember the former temple? Let's say they were 10 years old at **607 B.C.E.**, when Jerusalem was supposedly destroyed. Then in 520 B.C.E., we have many who are **97 years old**—who had to undertake the journey of four months and 900 miles!

To live to be 97 years old was rare even in those days:

> **Psalm 90:10; NWT:** The *span of our life is 70 years, or 80 if one is especially strong.* But they are filled with trouble and sorrow; They quickly pass by, and away we fly.

According to Ps 90:10, people in those days typically lived 70 years, or 80 if one was especially strong.

586/587 B.C.E. (76 years old)

Now, let's use 586/587 B.C.E. (which is stated by most scholars and sources) as the year when Jerusalem was destroyed. In that case, the situation described by Haggai and Ezra looks way more logical. Let's say these Israelites were 10 years old at **586/587 B.C.E.**, when Jerusalem was destroyed. Then in 520 B.C.E., we have many who are **76 years old**. This is more in line with Psalm 90:10.

70 Years of Desolation (80 years old)

Quoting from Jeremiah, the Watchtower also keeps stressing that Jerusalem laid desolate for 70 years.

> **Jer 29:10; NWT:** "For this is what Jehovah says, 'When 70 years at Babylon are fulfilled, I will turn my attention to you, and I will make good my promise by bringing you back to this place.'

Let's say again that these Israelites were 10 years old when Jerusalem was destroyed:

10 years old + 70 years of desolation = 80 years old when returning

Here, we have people **80 years old** returning to Jerusalem from Babylon. Using this simple reasoning, we have arrived at a similar age of the Israelites who saw the former temple in Jerusalem destroyed at 586/587 B.C.E. (**76 years old**).

607 B.C.E. or 586/587 B.C.E.?

So, which dating seems more in line with the other passages in the Bible? 607 B.C.E. or 586/587 B.C.E.? From our discussion we saw that 586/587 B.C.E. seems to be confirmed by the other passages from the Bible.

Just to compare, let's use the same calculation starting from 586/587 B.C.E. that most authorities use as the date when Jerusalem was destroyed:

> Counting 2,520 years from the destruction of Jerusalem in 586/587 B.C.E. takes us to 1893/1894 C.E.

> Nothing memorable happened in 1893/1894 C.E. from the standpoint of the Watchtower.

This discussion is by no means scholarly. It is apparently quite simplified. But sometimes simple is better.

Hopefully, the year 1914 is just a made-up fable and your family members are on their way off the shackles of the Watchtower. Next, you can explore together what the Watchtower wrote about the years 1799, 1872, 1874, 1914, 1918, 1925, 1975 etc. Since all this information is available online, I won't go into any details.

—— ··●·· ——

How Haggai Disproves 1914: Auxiliary Information

How the Watchtower Arrives at 1914

In case you don't know how the Watchtower calculates 2520 years from 607 B.C.E., to arrive at 1914 C.E., please find it below.

The calculations by the Watchtower combine: Daniel 4:10-17; Revelation 12:6, 14; Numbers 14:34; Ezekiel 4:6 in a following way, as quoted from the Watchtower magazine:

> "What do we see when we examine the prophetic pattern of Daniel 4:10-17? The giant, heaven-high tree represents divine rulership. The tree was cut down when God's Kingdom of Judah with its capital in Jerusalem fell in 607 B.C.E. After "seven times" of beastly rule by the nations passed, the two constraining bands of metal were released, and divine rulership was restored when Jesus Christ began to rule as King in God's heavenly government in 1914.

> A Day for a Year: This is how it is done: In Revelation chapter 12, verses 6 and 14, we learn that 1,260 days are equal to "a time [that is, 1 time] and times [that is, 2 times] and half a time," or a total of 3 1/2 times. So "a time" would be equal to 360 days. "Seven times" would be 360 multiplied by 7, or 2,520 days. Now if we count a day for a year, according to a Bible rule, the "seven times" equal 2,520 years. (Numbers 14:34; Ezekiel 4:6) Therefore, the duration of the "seven times," the Gentile Times, is from 607 B.C.E. to 1914 C.E." [w84 4/1 p. 7-8]

It takes a lot of faith to believe this explanation since the combination of these verses is just arbitrary. Anyway, this is the way one of JWs might write it down when explaining it to somebody else:

1260 days / 3.5 = 360 days (Re 12:6, 14)

360 days = "1 time" (1 year)

"7 times" should pass (Da 4:16)

7 × 360 = 2520 days, or years (Nu 14:34; Ezk 4:6)

2520 years from October 607 leads to October 1914

Comparison With 586/587 B.C.E.

Let's use the same calculation starting from 586/587 B.C.E. that most authorities use as the date when Jerusalem was destroyed.

2520 years from October 586/587 B.C.E. leads to October 1893/1894 C.E. Nothing breathtaking happened in 1893/1894 C.E., from the standpoint of the Watchtower.

About The Book of Haggai

The Watchtower publication *All Scripture Is Inspired of God and Beneficial* (*si pp. 166-168*) states:

Bible Book Number 37—Haggai

- Writer: Haggai
- Place Written: Jerusalem
- Writing Completed: 520 B.C.E.
- Time Covered: 112 days (520 B.C.E.)

About The Book of Ezra

The Watchtower publication *All Scripture Is Inspired of God and Beneficial* (*si pp. 85-87*) states:

Bible Book Number 15—Ezra

- Writer: Ezra
- Place Written: Jerusalem
- Writing Completed: c. 460 B.C.E.
- Time Covered: 537–c. 467 B.C.E.

— ••●•• —

Ruse: More Details

Briefly: We will see more details about Rahab, the Gibeonites, Jehu, Joseph, Rebekah, Laban and Leah. Get inspired how to use a ruse to make exit from JWs smooth for yourself and for your family.

Rahab

The Watchtower praises Rahab:

> **"Her ruse worked! ... Using a simple strategy, she had misdirected murderous men who had no right to the truth and she had saved innocent servants of Jehovah."** [w13 11/1 p. 14-15; emphasis added]

The example of Rahab is extremely important. If you have not read it from your Bible, please read it now below. After that, we will bring in more examples of ruse from the Bible.

Joshua, chapter 2 : 1 Joshua the son of Nun secretly sent two men out of Shittim as spies, saying, "Go, view the land, including Jericho." They went and came into the house of a prostitute whose name was Rahab, and slept there. 2 The king of Jericho was told, "Behold, men of the children of Israel came in here tonight to spy out the land." 3 Jericho's king sent to Rahab, saying, "Bring out the men who have come to you, who have entered into your house; for they have come to spy out all the land." 4 *The woman took the two men and hid them. Then she said, "Yes, the men came to me, but I didn't know where they came from. 5 About the time of the shutting of the gate, when it was dark, the men went out. Where the men went, I don't know. Pursue them quickly. You may catch up with them." 6 But she had brought them up to the roof, and hidden them under the stalks of flax which she had laid in order on the roof.* 7 The men pursued them along the way to the fords of the Jordan River. As soon as those who pursued them had gone out, they shut the gate. 8 Before they had lain down, she came up to them on the roof. 9 She said to the men, "I know that Yahweh has given you the land, and that the fear of you has fallen upon us, and that all the inhabitants of the land melt away before you. 10 For we have heard how Yahweh dried up the water of the Red Sea before you, when you came out of Egypt; and what you did to the two kings of the Amorites, who were beyond the Jordan, to Sihon and to Og, whom you utterly destroyed. 11 As soon as we had heard it, our hearts melted, and there wasn't any more spirit in any man, because of you: for Yahweh your God, he is God in heaven above, and on earth beneath. 12 Now therefore, please swear to me by Yahweh, since I have dealt kindly with you, that you also will deal kindly with my father's house, and give me a true sign; 13 and that you will save alive my father, my mother, my brothers, and my sisters, and all that they have, and will deliver our lives from death." 14 The men said to her, "Our life for yours, if you don't talk about this business of ours; and it shall be, when Yahweh gives us the land, that we will deal kindly and truly with you." 15 Then she let them down by a cord through the window; for her house was on the side of the wall, and she lived on the wall. 16 She said to them, "Go to the mountain, lest the pursuers find you. Hide yourselves there three days, until the pursuers have returned. Afterward, you may go your way." 17 The men said to her, "We will be guiltless of this your oath which you've made us to swear. 18 Behold, when we come into the land, tie this line of scarlet thread in the window which you used to let us down. Gather to yourself into the house your father, your mother, your brothers, and all your father's household. 19 It shall be that whoever goes out of the doors of your house into the street, his blood will be on his head, and we will be guiltless. Whoever is with you in the house, his blood shall be on our head, if any hand is on him. 20 But if you talk about this business of ours, then we shall be guiltless of your oath which you've made us to swear." 21 She said, "Let it be as you have said." She sent them away, and they departed. Then she tied the scarlet line in the window." [Joshua 2:1–21; *WEB*]

Joshua, chapter 6 : 17 The city shall be devoted, even it and all that is in it, to Yahweh. Only Rahab the prostitute shall live, she and all who are with her in the house, because she hid the messengers that we sent. 22 Joshua said to the two men who had spied out the land, "Go into the prostitute's house, and bring the woman and all that she has out from there, as you swore to her." 23 The young men who were spies went in, and brought out Rahab with her father, her mother, her brothers, and all that she had. They also brought out all of her relatives, and they set them outside of the camp of Israel. 24 They burned the city with fire, and all that was in it. Only they put the silver, the gold, and the vessels of bronze and of iron into the treasury of Yahweh's house. 25 But Rahab the prostitute, her father's household, and all that she had, Joshua saved alive. She lives in the middle of Israel to this day, because she hid the messengers whom Joshua sent to spy out Jericho. [Joshua 6:17, 22–25; *WEB*]

Ruse: More Examples

There are many more examples of ruse in the Bible that are also praised in the Watchtower literature. Let's see some more of them. Please, read these stories from your Bible and think what you can take from them to protect yourself and your loved ones by using a ruse until your spouse and family members are safely out of the Watchtower.

Gibeonites

Resorting to a ruse, the Gibeonites sent representatives who posed as travelers from a distant land:

"You likely know that Gibeon came to prominence soon after Joshua led Israel into the Promised Land and defeated Jericho. The Canaanites of Gibeon realized that they could not withstand Israel, who clearly had divine backing. What to do? **Resorting to a ruse, the Gibeonites sent representatives who posed as travelers from a distant land.** This effort toward peace succeeded, for Israel made a covenant with them. When their trick was exposed, the Gibeonites became gatherers of wood and drawers of water. God must not have been displeased with these people who sought peace. He supported Joshua's defense of the Gibeonites when they were attacked by five kings. Jehovah even performed the miracle of extending daylight for that battle.?—Joshua 9:3-27; 10:1-14." [w92 4/15 p. 32; *Gibeonites—They Sought Peace*]

Jehu

By the ruse of calling a great gathering for the worship of Baal, Jehu got all of Israel's Baal worshipers to assemble at the house of Baal. This way Jehu annihilated Baal out of Israel:

"Next, **by the ruse of calling a great gathering for the worship of Baal**, Jehu got all of Israel's Baal worshipers to assemble at the house of Baal. After ascertaining that there were no worshipers of Jehovah present, Jehu commanded his men to put to death everyone in the house. They thereafter destroyed the sacred pillars of Baal and pulled down the house, setting it aside for privies, for which the site was used down to the day of Jeremiah, writer of the account in the book of Kings. The record reads: "Thus Jehu annihilated Baal out of Israel." (2Ki 10:18-28)." [it-2 pp. 22-25; *Jehu*]

111

Joseph

Joseph had his silver cup placed in Benjamin's bag, which was part of his ruse:

"As on the previous visit, Joseph had each one's money put back in his bag (Ge 42:25), and additionally he had his silver cup placed in Benjamin's bag. After they had got under way, he had them overtaken and charged with stealing his silver cup. Perhaps to impress upon them its great value to him and the serious nature of their supposed crime, the man over Joseph's house was to say to them: "Is not this the thing that my master drinks from and by means of which he expertly reads omens?" (Ge 44:1-5) Of course, since **all of this was part of a ruse**, there is no basis for believing that Joseph actually used the silver cup to read omens. Apparently Joseph wanted to represent himself as an administrator of a land to which true worship was foreign." [it-2 pp. 106-112; *Joseph*]

Laban and Leah

Laban used a ruse with Jacob by giving him Leah as a wife instead of Rachel. Leah consented to be a part of this ruse:

"Leah became Jacob's first wife because, at night, Laban deceived Jacob by giving him Leah as a wife instead of Rachel, whom Jacob loved. Jacob protested his being tricked, but Laban argued that it was not the custom of the place to give the younger daughter in marriage before the firstborn. Leah likely was veiled, in keeping with the ancient Oriental custom of heavily veiling a prospective bride, and **this doubtless contributed to the success of the ruse**. Jacob had served seven years with Rachel in mind, but for this work he received Leah. Rachel was granted to him after he celebrated a week of seven days with Leah, but Jacob had to work seven more years to pay for Rachel."—Ge 29:18-28." [it-2 p. 229; *Leah*]

Rebekah

Rebekah disguises Jacob so that Jacob secures the blessing from his father for himself:

"The Bible does not say whether Isaac knows that Esau must serve Jacob. In any case, both Rebekah and Jacob know that the blessing belongs to him. Rebekah springs into action on hearing that Isaac intends to bless Esau when he takes his father a dish of game. The decisiveness and zeal that characterized her in her youth have not deserted her. She 'commands' Jacob to bring her two kids of goats. She will prepare a dish her husband is fond of. Then Jacob must impersonate Esau to obtain the blessing. Jacob objects. His father is bound to become aware of the **ruse** and curse him! Rebekah insists. "Upon me be the malediction meant for you, my son," she says. Then she makes the dish, **disguises Jacob**, and sends him to her husband.—Genesis 27:1-17. Why Rebekah acts this way is not stated. Many condemn her action, but the Bible does not, nor does Isaac on discovering that Jacob has received the blessing. Rather, Isaac amplifies it. (Genesis 27:29; 28:3, 4) **Rebekah** knows what Jehovah foretold about her sons. So she **acts to see that Jacob secures the blessing that is rightfully his. This is clearly in harmony with Jehovah's will.**—Romans 9:6-13." [w04 4/15 pp. 8-11; *Rebekah—A Godly Woman of Action*]

To Sum Up

Think about how to use a ruse to leave JWs together with your family.

—— ••●•• ——

Before the End of the Book

About Dan Bergher

This book was written for you, to make your life better. Still, you should know a little bit about me. As I am not that important, I am putting this part at the end of the book. I was one of Jehovah's Witnesses for 25 years, a time long enough to see some significant doctrinal changes within the organization. I grew up on a farm in the country with no religion or any religious inclinations around me. As I was growing up, I started reading a lot and thinking about the world around me, and I wanted a good world for everybody. So when I was told that Jehovah God would end this system of things and replace it with his Kingdom, I was excited. I wanted to believe in such a wonderful God.

The bookworm that I am, I started devouring books and publications from JWs. Those who conducted the Bible Study with me had it easy. A year after my baptism, I was an eager Ministerial Servant (a junior servant position within JWs) who was more than willing to do anything to advance the interests of JWs. Two years after my baptism, I was already an elder (a senior servant position within JWs) who always did way more than was required. The brothers and sisters loved my enthusiastic public talks since I presented not only the information but also my heart, overflowing with love for God and for the brothers and sisters.

In Bethel

Just three years after my baptism, I was invited to serve as a translator in Bethel (Headquarters of JWs). I translated from English but I didn't write in English. I am not a native English speaker and English is not my mother tongue, which you have probably noticed while reading this book. I hope that everything was clear, even though the style could have been more polished. What I am absolutely sure of is the fact that I did my best to reach out to your heart and help you do things in the best possible way.

My Bethel service lasted for three years; I was asked to leave Bethel once I announced my intention to get married. With my dear wife, we continued as full time servants for many more years until I was disfellowshipped after 25 years in the organization because I did not agree with some of the main teachings of JWs. I used many of the approaches described in this book with my wife. We left together with my wife, and our two children never became members of this organization.

114

A few months after my "departure" from JWs I started translating materials that would help JWs who were on their way out of the organization and I also started writing and giving away many of my own materials.

Exit Counseling

The focus of my work was personal exit counseling. Hundreds of brothers and sisters were writing to me, calling me and turning to me for help. I never turned anybody down, devoting more time to help them than when I served as a regular pioneer within JWs. These were hundreds of our dear brothers and sisters, hundreds of happy stories and hundreds of improved lives and saved marriages.

I was giving so much that it took to the point of a physical breakdown. It was then when several of my closest friends started telling me: "You must write a book; this way you can help more people than when you do it personally, only." It took several years before I heeded their advice to sit down and write the book that you are just reading.

Some who leave JWs decide to consult their life matters with professional therapists and medical professionals. I hope that this book will help you in many ways but it is by no means a substitute for any professional therapy.

In this book, I draw from my many years of **personal exit counseling** and from many courses on **self-help approaches** that I attended. Some of these are included in this book. I hope all this will help you make a smooth exit yourself while keeping your loved ones on your side and your family stronger than ever before.

Abbreviations

ASV – *American Standard Version* of the Holy Bible from 1901

Diaglott – *The Emphatic Diaglott New Testament* (Greek–English literal translation by Benjamin Wilson), still printed by the Watchtower

ESV – *The English Standard Version* of the Bible

g – *Awake!*, a magazine published by the Watchtower

HCSB – *The Holman Christian Standard Bible*

Insight – *Insight on the Scriptures*, a book published by the Watchtower

INT – *The Kingdom Interlinear Translation of the Greek Scriptures* produced by the Watchtower, also available online at www.jw.org

it – *Insight on the Scriptures*, a book published by the Watchtower

JW – Jehovah's Witness (one member)

JWs – Jehovah's Witnesses (as a group)

km – *Our Kingdom Ministry* , a publication from the Watchtower

ks – *Pay Attention to Yourselves and to All the Flock*, a publication for the elders from the Watchtower

KJV – *King James Version* of the Holy Bible

KJV+ – *King James Version* of the Holy Bible with Strong's numbers

NIV – *The New International Version* of the Bible

NWT – *New World Translation of the Holy Scriptures*

w – *The Watchtower*, a magazine published by the Watchtower

WEB – *The World English Bible*, Public Domain, not copyrighted translation. The World English Bible is a 1997 revision of the *American Standard Version* of the Holy Bible, first published in 1901.

WT – Watchtower, organization

YLT – *Young's Literal Translation of the Bible*

— ··•·· —

In a Nutshell: Basic Principles for a Smooth Exit

The principles below are mainly for those who want to exit from JWs and want to keep their JW spouse, their JW family members and their loved ones on their side until they are ready to leave the Watchtower, too.

The Basic Principles for a Smooth Exit

Choose your exit strategy: (1) Keep a low profile; (2) Stay in as inactive; (3) Fade out; (4) Get disfellowshipped; (5) Disassociate yourself.

When in doubt, leave it out: If you are *not sure* whether you should say something or do something, better *put it off*. There is usually no danger in postponing things. Sometimes you will postpone things for just a few minutes, at other times, you can leave it out for months.

Don't be viewed as an apostate: Once you become an apostate in your own family it will be extremely difficult to help your JW family members get out.

Threat of separation/divorce: Try honest, open communication. Ask friends for help. Consult with a professional.

You can stay in: You are in no danger if you are staying within the organization of JWs with all the facts you know. In fact, you can help your JW family members much better if you are viewed as a JW member, too.

Use a ruse: Follow the example of Rahab, Rebekah, Gibeonites, Jehu, Joseph, Laban and Leah. Misdirect those who have no right to the truth—to save yourself, your loved ones and your relatives from the Watchtower.

Maintain the picture of a faithful member: Do everything possible to look like a faithful member. Think about what the elders need to see to view you as a faithful member (although a "weaker" one). This way you will be able to help your loved ones get out of the Watchtower much better.

Turn in your report: Do it reliably each month, e.g. through somebody, over SMS or email to avoid unnecessary contact with the elders. It might be better to report several hours, rather than just the absolute minimum.

Meetings: You can skip most, and attend only such a meeting where you will be the least visible.

No doctrines: Be careful discussing the changes in doctrines, the changes of the "new light". As long as your spouse or your family members accept the authority of the "governing body" they will always have some explanation for these changes in the teachings of JWs: "The brothers know better."

Governing body: Focus on one single, weakest point: No central authority ("governing body") existed in Jerusalem or anywhere else at the beginning of the Christian congregation. Apostle Paul had its base in Antioch, not in Jerusalem. When it comes to the issue of circumcision as discussed in Acts chapter 15, a large gathering is described. This consisted of the apostles, older men (elders), Paul and Barnabas, who were traveling missionaries, and others. The decision in Acts 15 to send chosen men to Antioch was made by (1) the apostles and (2) the elders, (3) together with the whole congregation. (Ac 15:22) Thus, the decision was not made by a small "body" of men, but it was made by dozens, "together with the whole congregation"—which could mean that "the whole congregation" (men and women, brothers and sisters) made something like a resolution to show that they were in agreement with this decision. This large group combined to decide on an important issue affecting the local congregations. This is the sole Bible example of brothers convening to decide on an issue. See the Appendix.

First you, your spouse and family: First, help out of the Watchtower your spouse, your family and your loved ones. Only and only then, try helping other brothers and sisters to get out.

Read the Bible chronologically together: The best way to see there was no central authority ("governing body") in the first century C.E., is to read the Bible chronologically, together, as a family. Focus on the book of Acts.

Children: Do your best to keep putting their baptism off.

Interested one: Remain safe as an interested person. Don't get baptized as one of JWs. This way you can help your JW family members the best.

Make new friends: Once you leave the Watchtower, you will lose all your friends. Prepare for that. Start making new friends not to end up alone.

Add important points relevant to your own situation:

. . . .

. . . .

. . . .

My Three ToDo's

Please, write down your three most important action points at this time.
Note down today's date.
Write down a date to revisit these points and decide on new ones.

1. ....

2. ....

3. ....

Date today: ....

Date to revisit: ....

✳ Taking My Time to Reflect <Ask 10–100 times>

The most helpful questions from the whole book to reflect on.

- What will create more here? For me, my spouse, my family, for ...
- How can I make this as easy as possible? For me, my spouse, my family.
- Which approach (steps) will create more?
- What possibilities are there?
- What could work here?
- What other questions can help me?
- Which approach/decision feels lighter/heavier?
- Which approach/decision feels expanding/limiting?

Before You Go: Did You Like This Book?

How did this book help you? Please, let everyone know by posting a review on Amazon. These shortened links will take you directly to:

Reviews Page: http://bit.ly/exitmanualreview | bit.ly/exitmanualreview

Book Page: http://bit.ly/exitmanualjws | bit.ly/exitmanualjws

<You can leave out "http://">

Thank you very much.

More Support

For more support, go to **www.FreeFlowPal.com**

What you will find here:

- Links to maps of Apostle Paul's Journeys, to chronological Bibles and other books to help you.
- Free download of the best Chronological Bible Reading Plan in PDF.
- Free tips and encouragement.

Made in the USA
Middletown, DE
21 March 2023

27337710R00076